MAKING MARBLE-ACTION GAMES, GADGETS MAZES & CONTRAPTIONS

Designs for 10 Outlandish, Ingenious and Intricate Woodworking Projects

MAKING MARBLE-ACTION GAMES, GADGETS MAZES & CONTRAPTIONS

Designs for 10 Outlandish, Ingenious and Intricate Woodworking Projects

Alan and Gill Bridgewater

STACKPOLE
BOOKS

Copyright © 1999 Stackpole Books

Published by
STACKPOLE BOOKS
5067 Ritter Road
Mechanicsburg, PA 17055
www.stackpolebooks.com

Printed in the United States of America

10 9 8 7 6 5 4 3 2

FIRST EDITION

Cover design by Wendy Reynolds
Cover and interior color photographs by Ian Parsons
Interior line drawings and black-and-white photographs by the authors

RUBE GOLDBERG is a registered trademark of Rube Goldberg, Inc.

The Magnificent Goldberg-Robinson-Williamson Marble-Kicking Device is a suggested project by the authors and is not in whole or in part a product licensed or endorsed by Rube Goldberg, Inc.

Library of Congress Cataloging-in-Publication Data

Bridgewater, Alan.
    Making marble-action games, gadgets, mazes & contraptions: designs for 10 outlandish, ingenious and intricate woodworking projects / Alan and Gill Bridgewater.
       p.   cm.
    ISBN 0–8117–2855–2
    1. Wooden toy making. 2. Wooden boxes. 3. Maze puzzles. 4. Marbles (Game) I. Bridgewater, Gill. II. Title.
TT174.5.W6B7277   1999
745.592—dc21   99–11796
                                        CIP

We dedicate this book to our grandfathers, and to all the other amateur inventors and unbolt-and-poke-around artists of the 1930s and '40s who had no choice but to make do and mend. They couldn't phone up a help line when their steam radios and gas freezers went down, or throw away their motorcycles when a wheel needed a new bearing. They simply rolled up their sleeves and took a stab at solving the problems. We truly admire these wonderfully ingenious and self-sufficient folks. No doubt they would have enjoyed making the projects in this book.

Contents

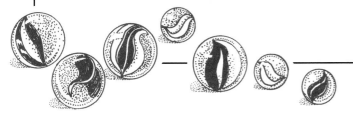

Acknowledgments

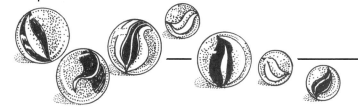

We would like to thank all the manufacturers who have over the years supplied us with the best of the best: Tim Effrem, President, Wood Carvers Supply (wood carving tools); Jim Brewer, Research and Marketing Manager, Freud (forstner drill bits); John P. Jodkin, Vice President, Delta International Machine Corp. (band saws); Dawn Fretz, Marketing Assistant, De-Sta-Co. (clamps); Paragon Communications, Evo-Stick (PVA adhesive).

Most of all, we would like to thank Friedrich Wilhelm Emmerich, of E. C. Emmerich Planes in Remscheid, Germany, for his beautiful wooden planes. They are special! If you want to set yourself up with the best of all modern planes, these are the ones to go for.

Last but not least, we would like to thank our editor, Kyle Weaver of Stackpole Books, for brainstorming the idea for this book.

Introduction

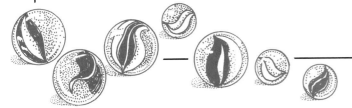

This book draws its inspiration from, and pays tribute to, two of the most lovable and quirky characters of our time: William Heath Robinson (1872–1944), who lived in England, and Rube Goldberg (1883–1970), who lived in the United States. Both were gifted artists whose cartoons beautifully illustrate semilunatic labor-saving devices that expose the crazy, slightly unzipped nature of our machine age.

When I was a kid, the names "Heath Robinson" and "Rube Goldberg" were used derisively to describe notions that, though designed to be modern and labor saving, were all too obviously foolish and absurd. So, when the guy next door had in mind to power his car by the methane gas given off by his prize pet pig, or a packaging expert came up with an idea to spin hens around at speed so they would lay flat, easy-to-pack eggs, the adults around me would knowingly tap the side of the head, roll the eyes, raise the eyebrows, and mutter, "What a Rube" or "What a Heath Robinson."

What Heath Robinson and Rube Goldberg illustrations bring home to us is that the high-flown, new-fangled notions of the machine age are inherently flawed by the fact that they all too often ignore the human condition. When I read that the world's biggest airport has been closed down because of "circumstances beyond our control," I begin to make up bizarre, Robinson- and Goldberg-type explanations such as this: The disgruntled wife of an airport maintenance man gives her husband tuna sandwiches for lunch. He hates fish, so he flushes the sandwiches down the toilet. The toilet becomes blocked and overflows, flooding a basement under the main airport control tower, so that the mice are forced to move to higher ground. An enterprising mouse sets up home in the back of a computer,

the computer closes down, and before you can say "Heath Robinson" or "Rube Goldberg," the airport is at a standstill. The absolute stupidity of such situations gives most of us a warm, feel-good burst of pleasure. It's as if we're comforted and reassured by the knowledge that we aren't alone in our vulnerability and stupidity.

Heath Robinson's cartoons are densely populated by characters busy winding handles, pulling strings, and yanking levers, all in an effort to operate labor-saving devices. Of course, it's contrary and ridiculous to have miles of string, lots of pulleys, and all manner of levers, springs, and mirrors, all to boil an egg or rock a cradle, but that's precisely what's so humorous. Some of his funniest cartoons have to do with a lunatic, do-it-the-most-difficult-way inventor named Professor Branestawm. If you think of a cross between the German-American rocket scientist Wernher von Braun and Albert Einstein, and throw in a dash of Monty Python, you won't be far wrong.

Rube Goldberg also created cartoons of all manner of daft and dippy devices that were designed to perform simple tasks. He came up with a character called Professor Lucifer Gorgonzola Butts. His cartoons are filled with nutty fruitcake guys and animals and lots of tubes, wires, and strings. The various details in the cartoon are very seriously labeled with letters, numbers, and captions.

One little beauty has to do with the brilliant design for a self-opening umbrella. It shows a sort of laboratory setup, with a dried prune at one end and a guy under a closed umbrella at the other. The sequence of cause-and-effect events goes like this: Raindrops fall on a dried prune, causing the prune to swell up and push against a lever. The lever operates an iron hand that rubs a wheel against a flint, which sends off a shower of sparks to ignite a candle. The flame sets a kettle boiling, and the steam blows a whistle. A circus monkey thinks that the whistle is his signal to jump on a trapeze. The swinging trapeze causes a knife to cut a cord, releasing a balloon, which pulls a string that releases a flock of birds that are tied to the spokes of the umbrella, thus opening the umbrella.

Just in case you are wondering what all this has to do with the subject of this book, the answer is delightfully simple. Just like the Heath Robinson Rube Goldberg devices, all the projects in this book are nonsensical, absurd, nonproductive, and altogether anarchic and slightly cuckoo. Okay, so the woodworking techniques are exciting, the finished projects are beautiful, and the movements are dynamic, but what, you might ask, is the benefit of making these projects? Well, of course, the pleasure you gain from the thought processes, the designing, and the doing. You might simply think of the projects as being kinetic sculptures or adult toys. Or then again, you could consider them experiments in what Robinson and Goldberg might have described as "the science of marble transference and the relationship between rolling balls, level and sloping planes, and primary mechanical movements."

Or, as my grandfather used to say, "Most of the fun is in the doing."

Getting Started

Making the Basic Box

What many beginners to woodworking fail to understand is that making a box is, in many ways, just about as difficult as woodworking gets. It's not that the overall form is especially complex, nor that there are so many component parts that it's hard to figure out how they relate to each other; it's only that each part must be painstakingly cut and worked so that all faces are true. What we mean by "true" is at 90-degree angles or at right angles. If you fail to plane each component part so that it is true, with all sides and edges being at crisp right angles to one another, the box is going to be less than perfect and you are going to be disappointed.

Please do not rush making the boxes. Enjoy the various procedures. Spend time scraping and sanding, and when you think it's ready, spend a little more time.

As shown in the working drawings throughout the book, the basic box is made from six component parts: two long sides, two short sides, a base, and a lid. One short side is cut for the slot, long sides are rabbeted at the ends to take the short sides, and all four sides are rabbeted and grooved to take the plywood base and the clear plastic sliding lid. The basic section from which all the sides are made measures ⅜ inch thick and 2 inches wide. It has a 3/16-by-3/16-inch rabbet running with the grain along the bottom edge and two ⅛-by-⅛-inch grooves plowed on the inside face. Though the same basic section is used for all the boxes, it is sometimes modified by reducing the 2-inch width to 1¾

inches. You have a choice: You can go for a full-depth two-groove box or a shallower one-groove box, depending on the project. To fit the lid, whether it's plywood or a clear plastic sheet, the groove on one short side is modified so that it becomes a through slot.

We decided to add variety by using two contrasting woods: American oak for the pale boxes and English brown oak for the dark streaked brown boxes. We like to use traditional hand tools such as planes and scrapers and describe how to make the projects using such tools, but you can use routers and machine planers if you prefer.

Squaring the Wood

1. Keeping in mind that the success of the box depends on the accuracy at the preparation stage, take your carefully chosen length of sawn wood, at a little over ½ inch thick and 2¼ inches wide, and check it over for potential problems. Avoid wood that is split or knotty. Select the best side, and use a smoothing plane to work that side to a smooth finish (see Fig. 1). The best procedure is to hold the workpiece on the bench using stops or dogs, and repeatedly check with a metal straightedge. Pencil-label this face with a "face side" mark that points to the "face edge."

2. Mount the wood in the vise with the face edge uppermost, and use the plane of your choice to work the edge square to the face side (see Fig. 2). Repeatedly check with a metal straightedge and a metal square.

1

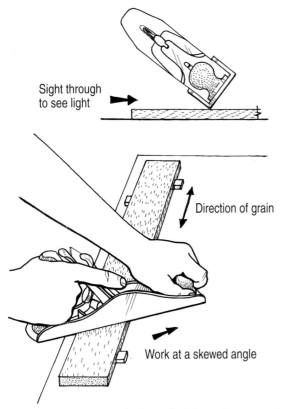

Sight through
to see light

Direction of grain

Work at a skewed angle

Fig. 1. (Bottom) Starting at the far end of the workpiece, make cuts at a skewed sliding angle to the run of the grain. (Top) Tilt the plane on its side and test for irregularities—dips and peaks—by sighting between the edge of the plane and the workpiece.

3. Set the marking gauge to the width of the wood—in this case 2 inches—and drag a gauged line around all faces and edges.

4. Shade in the waste with a pencil so you can see clearly what needs to be cut away. Mount the workpiece in the vise with the waste uppermost, and plane back to the gauged line. Once again, check with the metal rule and square.

5. Set the gauge to ⅜ inch and run a gauged line right around the wood (see Fig. 3).

6. Rerun, working with the smooth plane, and bring the other face down to the gauged line as before, only this time check after every few cuts.

Cutting the Grooves and the With-Grain Rabbet

1. When you have achieved a good length of true squared wood at 2 inches wide and ⅜ inch thick, with the face side and face edge clearly marked, take your grooving plane—we used an old Record 044 plow plane—and fit it out with a ⅛-inch cutter.

2. Set the fence to ¼ inch and the depth gauge foot to ⅛ inch.

3. Clamp the length of wood with the face side down on the bench, and run the first groove ¼ inch from the face edge. Work from the end of the wood farthest away from you and then gradually back up. The groove needs to finish up at ⅛ inch wide and ⅛ inch deep.

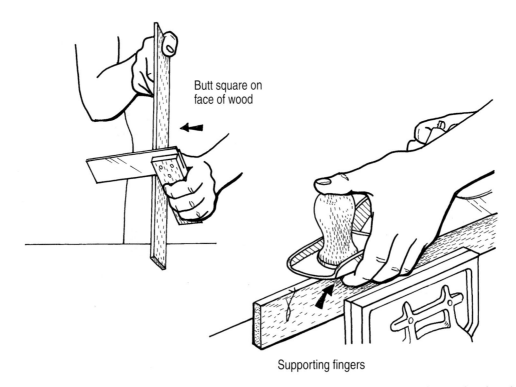

Butt square on
face of wood

Supporting fingers

Fig. 2. (Left) Check with a square, and mark any high spots with a pencil. (Right) Apply pressure with your thumb and use your fingers as a guide. Use the other hand to supply the forward thrust.

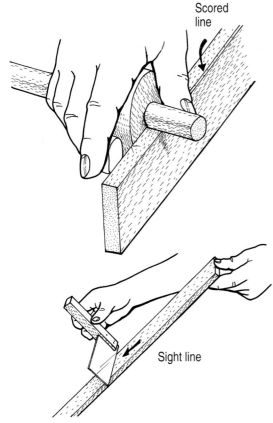

Scored line

Sizing the Lengths

1. When you have achieved a good length of box section, complete with two grooves and an edge rabbet, take the bench hook and a small crosscut saw and cut the wood to length (see Fig. 5). You need four lengths for each box you want to make, two at 10½ inches and two at 7 inches. This allows for a good amount of cutting waste.

2. Take the square, rule, and marking knife, and measure the sides to the precise length. Allowing for waste to be cut back at both ends, the long sides need to be marked out at 10 inches and the short sides at 6⅝ inches.

3. The next step is to plane the sawn ends back square. This can be achieved in any number of ways: in

Sight line

Fig. 3. (Top) Set the gauge fence on the face side of the wood and score the lines around the edges. (Bottom) Test for general unevenness by holding the square across the workpiece and sighting down the wood. If all is well, the band of light that shines under the straightedge will be thin, straight, and parallel.

4. When you are happy with the first groove, reset the fence to ⅝ inch and plow the other groove (see Fig. 4).

5. Finally, turn the wood around so that you can work the other edge on the same face, and fit the 3/16-inch cutter. Set the fence hard up against the body of the plane, set the depth stop foot to about 3/16 inch, and run a rabbet along the edge of the wood.

Special Tip

If you plan to make lots of little boxes and you don't want to work with machines but you do want to keep your costs to a minimum, get one of the old, out-of-production Stanley or Record plow planes. Sold with a range of cutters running from ⅛ to 9/16 inch, these planes can be used to work everything from grooves and tongues to stepped architrave profiles and rabbets. Such a plane can be picked up at a flea market for less than the cost of a modern electric router cutter.

Fig. 4. Plowing the grooves. Make sure all along the way that the fence—held in the left hand—is pushed hard up against the face edge of the workpiece. If all is well, the grooves will be ⅛ inch wide, ⅛ inch deep, and ¼ inch apart.

Fig. 5. Butt the workpiece hard up against the bench hook stop, sight down the saw, hold it against the side of the stop, and then make the cut.

Fig. 6. Shooting the sawn end. Note how the workpiece is butted hard up against a piece of waste to prevent the grain from splitting out.

the vise and working from both edges, in the vise with supporting blocks along the edges to help avoid splitting the grain, and so on. One of the swiftest traditional methods is to use a plane in conjunction with an easy-to-make apparatus known as a shooting board ramp. All this is, in effect, is a long bench hook with a paral-

lel ramp added to the side. The workpiece is butted against a piece of waste and hard up against the stop, and then a plane is set on its side and run at speed down the ramp so that it skims a shaving off the end of the workpiece.

4. Place the workpiece firmly against a piece of waste of similar thickness—I'm using a piece left over from another side strip—and use a plane to shoot the end (see Fig. 6). The waste piece prevents the grain from splitting out.

5. Repeat the procedure until you halve the gauged line, then turn the wood around and shoot the other end.

Cutting the Rabbet

1. Though the unnailed rabbeted or lapped housing joint has little or no glue strength—it wouldn't be any good for, say, a drawer or a heavy-duty chest—it's strong enough for a small box like this.

2. Study the working drawings throughout the book. Then take the long sides and use a rule, square, and knife to set out the ⅜-inch-wide rabbets. Do this on the inside box face on both ends of both long sides.

3. Set the marking gauge to 3/16 inch, and gauge around the edges and ends of the wood. Shade in the areas that need to be lowered.

4. With the workpiece butted up firmly against the bench hook, take a small backsaw and run the shoulder cut to the waste side of the scored line (see Fig. 7).

Fig. 7. Cutting the shoulder of the rabbet. Note the white, precut jig strip used to help align the cut.

5. With the workpiece still butted in the bench hook, use a rabbet plane to lower the waste to the gauged line (see Fig. 8). Note how I use the end of the bench hook stop and the end of the piece of waste to help me keep the plane on track.

6. Test-fit the pieces several times along the way (see Fig. 9). Mark the sides so that they can easily be matched up to their mates.

7. Decide which of the two short sides is to be slotted, then saw through the top slot and plane the sawn edges back to the mark. You should finish up with a slot ⅛ inch wide to match the top groove on the other three sides of the box (see Fig. 10).

Using a Scraper

1. For the best of all finishes—many times better than the finest abrasive papers—you can't beat using a cabinet scraper. Whereas sandpaper leaves the surface fuzzy and powdery, the scraper leaves the surface smooth and burnished—really beautiful! In the context of making this box, I decided to scrape the strips on the face side and the face edge.

2. Start by building a jig. Set the workpiece with the best face up on the bench, and enclose it with three pieces of thin wood nailed to the bench. In action, you slide the workpiece into the jig so that it is firm and butted against the end stop, and then make two or three passes with a scraper (see Fig. 11).

3. Build a jig to take a batch of sides, and scrape the face edges down to the same level (see Fig. 12).

Fig. 8. Hold the rabbet plane upright, and skim the waste down to the gauged line. The alignment is aided by running the side of the plane against the end of the stop.

Gluing and Clamping Up

1. Once the box's four sides have been grooved, rabbeted, and scraped to a perfect finish, test-fit the pieces together in a trial dry run. Cut waste pieces to set between the clamp heads and the workpiece, have the glue ready, have a damp cloth close to hand, select a spreading stick, and so on—everything except actually spreading on the glue.

Fig. 9. Check the fit and pencil-label the pieces so that the box can swiftly be put together the same way.

Fig. 10. One end has to be worked so that the groove becomes a slot to fit the clear plastic sheet used in most projects.

Fig. 11. Butt the workpiece hard up against the stop, and then run the scraper with a slightly skewed shearing action. If the wood cuts up rough, try turning it around and working from the other direction.

Fig. 12. Scraping the sides in a sandwich is a good way to bring all the sides to the same height and the same degree of finish.

2. Put the four sides together in the order as planned, clamp them up just as you would if they had been glued, and test with the square (see Fig. 13).

3. If, as is likely, the four sides are out of square, then experiment with various clamping positions and tensions, with the clamps set at a skewed angle, to try to get the box square.

4. If you can't achieve squareness this way, skim the joints here and there for a good fit.

5. When you have achieved a fair degree of accuracy, undo the clamps, clear the working area of clutter, have a final check that all the tools and materials are at hand, and then systematically smear glue on mating faces and clamp up. Pay particular attention to the little strip of wood that sits above the slot—it's most important that it's correctly placed and that the slot is ⅛ inch wide.

6. After the glue has partially set, wipe the dribbles away with a knife or chisel and set aside for the glue to cure.

Fitting the Base and the Lid

1. When the glue has set, remove the clamps and clear the work surface of clutter.

2. Have another test with the square just to make sure that the frame hasn't twisted, then take a strip of ⅛-inch-thick plywood or a scrap of clear plastic sheet and test the slot and grooves (see Fig. 14). If there are glue blobs, or the width of the slot needs easing, now is the time to make adjustments.

3. Cut the ⅛-inch-thick plywood base sheet to size and clean up the edges. Determine, depending on the project you are working on, whether the base sheet must be fitted at this time or can be left to a later stage.

4. When you are ready to fit the base, set the sheet of plywood on the rabbet, drill little pilot holes through the ply and on into the box sides, tap the nails into place, and the box is made (see Fig. 15).

Cutting the Plywood

1. Take the sheet of ⅛-inch-thick plywood, and use a rule and pencil to establish one long edge.

2. Using a metal safety ruler and craft knife, score along the drawn line until you cut through. Four or five strokes should do the trick.

3. Measure along the true edge for the length of the sheet, then square off from these marks to establish the ends.

4. Finally, score along these lines, then measure and score for the last side.

Special Tip
Though the thin plywood can be cut with a handsaw, on a band saw, or even on a scroll saw, I have found that the best way is to use a safety ruler and knife. Just make sure that you do the scoring on a wooden board, with the safety ruler on the good side of the drawn line, so that the blade is to the waste side.

Fig. 13. Repeatedly adjust the tension of the clamps and test for squareness.

Fig. 14. Test the groove by sliding in a piece of waste plywood, paying particular attention to the corners nearest the slot.

Cutting the Clear Plastic Sheet

1. First let's make sure we are all talking about the same product. You need a rigid sheet of clear plastic, such as Perspex, acrylic, or polycarbonate, at about $3/16$ inch thick. The product comes with protective paper or plastic film on both sides.

2. Mark and score the sheet in much the same way as the plywood.

3. With the scored surface uppermost, align the score with the edge of the work surface and apply even downward pressure so as to snap along the scored line.

4. Finally, trim the edge with a block plane, remove the protective paper, and slide into place.

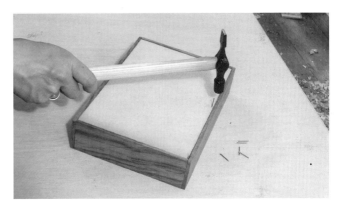

Fig. 15. Drill starter holes, tap the nails in, and punch the heads slightly below the surface.

Tool and Technique Tips

Sawing Along the Run of the Grain

If you want to cut a lot of your own wood to size, you'll need a ripsaw. A ripsaw is designed specifically to cut in line with the grain. The teeth are square cut, meaning that they don't have a bevel on the side face. In use, the teeth act like a series of chisels, with each tooth in line cutting its own little groove. If you want to cut down the length of the wood—down a plank or a strip—then a ripsaw is the tool for you. In use, the wood needs to be supported at a comfortable working height, so that your shoulder is behind the thrust of the saw and so that you can sight down the back of the blade (see Fig. 16).

If you plan to buy a new ripsaw, be sure to get the best—one with a wooden handle, made by an American, German, or English manufacturer. Don't be persuaded to by an all-purpose bargain saw; there is no such thing! If you want to follow tradition, you could do well to buy a nineteenth-century saw from a specialist tool supplier and have it looked over by a saw doctor.

Using a Gent's Saw with a Bench Hook

Secure the bench hook in the vise, push the workpiece hard up against the stop, set the saw to the waste side of the scored line, and use the toe of the blade to make a

Fig. 16. Use a ripsaw to cut along the grain.

few dragging strokes. When you have established the cut, sight down the back of the saw to ensure that the cut is on line, and use the full length of the blade to complete. Ease off the pressure toward completion so as not to split the grain when the saw exits (see Fig. 17).

Using a Marking Knife

The line of cut—meaning the line that will eventually need to be cut with a saw or chisel—should be marked out with a knife. Set the square down on the workpiece so that the metal straightedge is on the mark, position the knife hard up against the straightedge, and make the cut with a single dragging stroke. Though the photograph shows a small penknife, it's best, for greatest accuracy, to use a knife that has a bevel on one side only, so that the flat face of the blade can be run close to the edge (see Fig. 18).

Planing the Edge

The technique of planing the edges of boards true, straight, and square is termed jointing, because more often than not the object of the exercise is to plane two such boards and join them together edge to edge. Though on long lengths this procedure is best worked with the long-soled jointing plane, on short pieces it is best managed with the smoothing plane. Our favorite plane is the wooden Primus smoothing plane, made by E. C. E. in Germany. If you can afford only one plane, this is the one you should buy. It's comfortable to hold, perfectly balanced, and beautiful (see Fig. 19).

Fig. 17. Use a gent's saw in conjunction with a bench hook to cut across the run of the grain.

Fig. 18. Score an accurate cutting line with a knife and square.

Fig. 19. Use a smoothing plane to plane an edge.

Fig. 20. Planing end grain with a wooden block plane.

Fig. 21. Planing end grain on a ramp shooting board.

Planing End Grain

One way to plane end grain is to support the workpiece in the vise and run the plane with a slightly skewed shearing action. All you do is set the workpiece in the vise so that the end to be worked is uppermost, with a strip of waste at the runoff end, and start the run. If the waste piece is correctly placed, it will prevent the edge from splitting, as it will take the brunt of the runoff action (see Fig. 20).

Another technique of planing end grain is to use a shooting board. Here you place the workpiece firmly against the shooting board, with a piece of waste between it and the stop, set the plane on its side, and then run it down the ramp so that it skims the end of the workpiece to a good finish (see Fig. 21). Though the photograph shows a block plane, it's better to use a large plane, because the weight will give the stroke more momentum.

Shooting Long-Grain Cuts

The ramp shooting board can also be great for working long-grain cuts on short lengths of wood. The best procedure is to alternately shoot the workpiece with the face side up and then face side down, so as to minimize warping and to achieve the best finish. Using a shooting board with a ramp is a good time saver and ensures that more of the plane's cutting edge is used (see Fig. 22).

Fig. 22. Planing long grain on a ramp shooting board.

The Stanley 45 Combination Plane

If you enjoy making small boxes, and you want to cut tongues, grooves, rabbets, and moldings with planes rather than noisy, dust-making routers, then a Stanley 45 combination plane, or its copy, the Record 405, is a

good option. Though the Stanley and the Record are long out of production, they can easily be bought secondhand (see Fig. 23). In use, you fit the cutter of your choice, set the depth of cut, put the spurs down if you are cutting across the grain, make sure that the sledge runners are perfectly aligned with the side edge of the blade (see Fig. 24), set the fence, and you're ready to go.

The trick to using the 45 is being able to support the workpiece so that it overhangs the side of the bench. Though this is sometimes a bit tricky, especially when the workpiece is small, a holdfast or hold-down is very useful. Note how the workpiece is butted hard up against a stop (see Fig. 25). If you need to work a groove in end grain, the best procedure is to clamp a piece of waste wood at the runoff end to prevent the wood from splitting when the plane runs off the edge (see Fig. 26).

The secret to using the plane is to spend time tuning it to make the lightest of skimming cuts, and then to make a series of easy passes. So, for example, when you are cutting a deep groove, make light passes with your left hand pressing the fence hard up against the side of the board and your right hand supplying the push and the downward pressure. Start at the end farther away from you, and slowly back up so that the strokes become longer and you run over the previous cuts (see Fig. 27). If everything is just right—the plane is nicely tuned and the wood is free from knots—then the waste will come

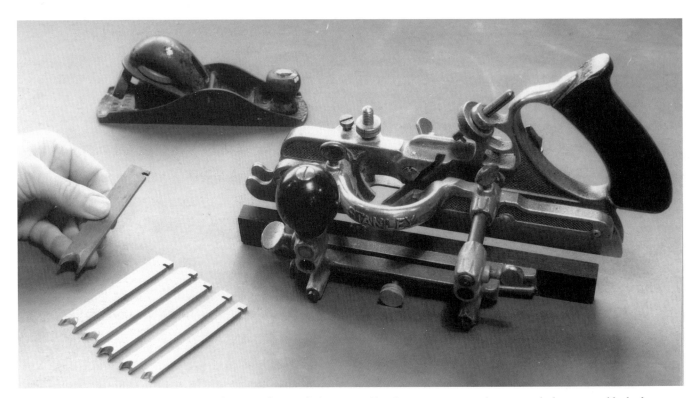

Fig. 23. The fabulous Stanley 45 combination plane with the range of bead cutters, compared in size with the average block plane.

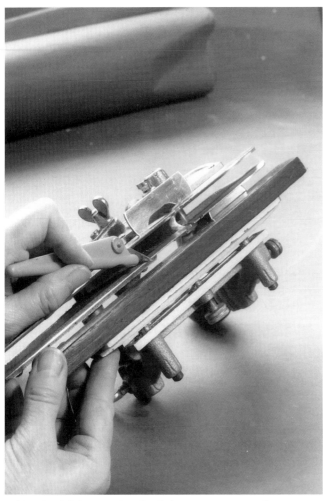

Fig. 24. Make sure that the sledge runners are in alignment.

Fig. 25. Using the Stanley 45 with the workpiece secured with a holdfast.

Fig. 26. Using the Stanley 45 to work end grain with the workpiece held in the vise and the waste piece being gripped with a sash clamp.

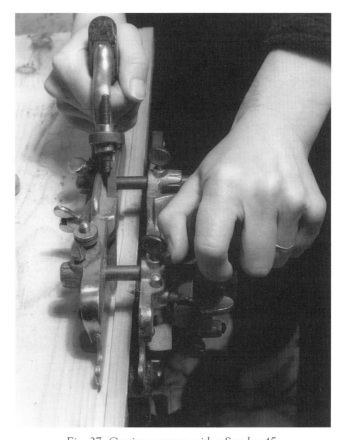

Fig. 27. Cutting a groove with a Stanley 45.

Fig. 28. Using a Stanley 45: the correct handholds and stance.

away as a continuous ribbon. No noise, no dust—just a beautiful, crisp cut (see Fig. 28).

Working on a Lathe

When working on a lathe, it's best to fit it up with a four-jaw chuck. Certainly, it does look a bit heavy—a bit like using a steamroller to crack a nut, maybe—but that said, it can be used to secure just about everything from a fairly large section down to a small knob (see Fig. 29). It's especially good for working small knobs and the like, because you can move the tailstock out of the way and approach the workpiece from the bed of the lathe. With this particular chuck, you can also hold rings and hollow forms by using the jaws in their expanding mode.

You need two tools for basic measuring: a pair of dividers for measuring step-offs and a pair of calipers for measuring diameters (see Fig. 30).

Drilling Small Holes

For drilling very small holes, of about $1/16$ inch diameter, the best tool is the old-fashioned spiral pump drill. Okay, so it's slow, but the bit can be set precisely on the mark. To make your own drill bits, take a suitable size nail, tap the end to an arrow point, tidy it up with a file, and mount it in the drill. No problem if it gets lost; you can simply make another (see Figs. 31 and 32).

Dowels

For the projects in this book, you'll need lots of small-diameter dowels. The easiest way of cutting a dowel to length, so that both ends are smooth and slightly rounded, is to mark the dowel to length and then repeatedly roll it under a knife. After three or four rolls, you will find that the dowel separates—perfectly cut, finished, and ready to use (see Fig. 33).

Fig. 29. A four-jaw lathe chuck is good for holding small items that need to be worked end-on.

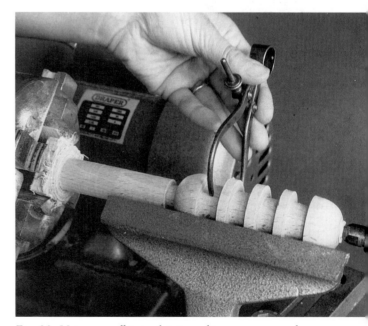

Fig. 30. Using a small pair of spring calipers to measure the diameter of the core, or waste wood at the center.

Fig. 31. Flatten the point of the nail on a metal block.

Fig. 32. Fit the homemade arrowhead bit in the drill.

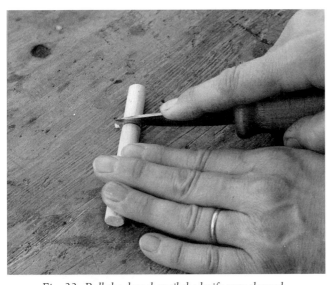

Fig. 33. Roll the dowel until the knife cuts through.

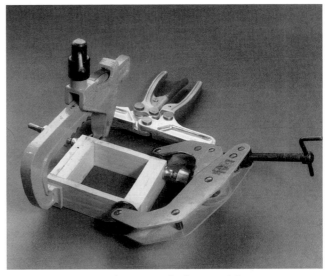

Fig. 34. Obtain a good selection of clamps.

Clamps

Making the projects is much easier if you have plenty of clamps to choose from. They don't have to be super-strong, but they should be well designed, with a range of different heads and screw actions so that they can be used in all kinds of tricky situations (see Fig. 34).

Project 1
....

Marble Coordination Tester

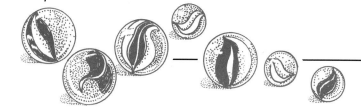

This marble game draws its inspiration from the penny-in-the-slot machines I used to play at fairgrounds, amusement arcades, and seaside piers when I was a kid. They were beautifully simple. All you did was put a penny in the slot, push a knob to deliver the ball, and then flick a lever to send the balls zooming around the track. The idea was to get the balls in the high-number pockets to achieve a top score.

There is no doubt that our Marble Coordination Tester is a fun-filled, nail-biting, finger-tingling endurance test—a real swine to play! It might look easy enough—after all, you only have to get the marbles in the pockets, and surely that can't be too difficult—but you can take it from us, it's a nerve-racking game to play. So if you want to make a game that is going to have you and your friends climbing the walls with frustration, then this is the project for you.

Design, Structure, and Techniques

Look over the project picture (see color section) and the working drawings (see Figs. 1-1, 1-2, and 1-3). You will need a box, as detailed in the section on Making the Basic Box, plus seven other component parts: the marble magazine with its five chambers, the baffle cross at the center, the four baffle walls, and the pocket plate. The magazine is cut from 1¼-inch-thick wood so that its top surface is just clear of the underside of the clear plastic sheet. Note the way the marble pockets are arranged within the pattern of baffles, so that once a marble is in place in a pocket, there is no room for another marble to pass. The whole idea of this arrangement is that the only way to successfully play is to start by filling the furthermost pockets. Keep this information under your hat!

The diameter of the marble pockets, and the thickness of the wood through which they are drilled, does to a great extent determine how firmly the marbles are fixed in their pockets. The thinner the wood and the smaller the diameter of the pockets, the easier it is to dislodge the marbles. After a lot of thought, we decided to go for ⅛-inch-thick ply for the base plate, with the pocket holes being ½ inch, ⅜ inch, and ¼ inch. The baffles need to have the grain running along their length, and the magazine needs to have the grain running across the thickness of the walls, so that the strength is at the bottom of the marble chambers.

The best tools for the job, if you have them, are an electric scroll saw for the fine fretwork and a pillar drill and a band saw to cut the thicker wood for the marble magazine. That said, if you enjoy using hand tools and don't mind going at a slow, easy pace, you can use a fretwork saw for the thin wood and a small frame bow saw—one with a wooden H frame—for the magazine.

Choosing the Wood

The best way to select wood is to look at the shape of the component part and consider how it is going to be worked and how thick it is going to wind up. Carefully consider how it is going to be placed in the general scheme of things. We decided to use ⅛-inch-thick ply for the base plate, a ¼-inch-thick piece of American cherry for the baffles, and a 1¼-inch-thick chunk of American oak for the marble magazine.

Making the Project
Cutting the Baffles

1. After carefully choosing your wood and making sure that it is free from splits and knots, plane it down

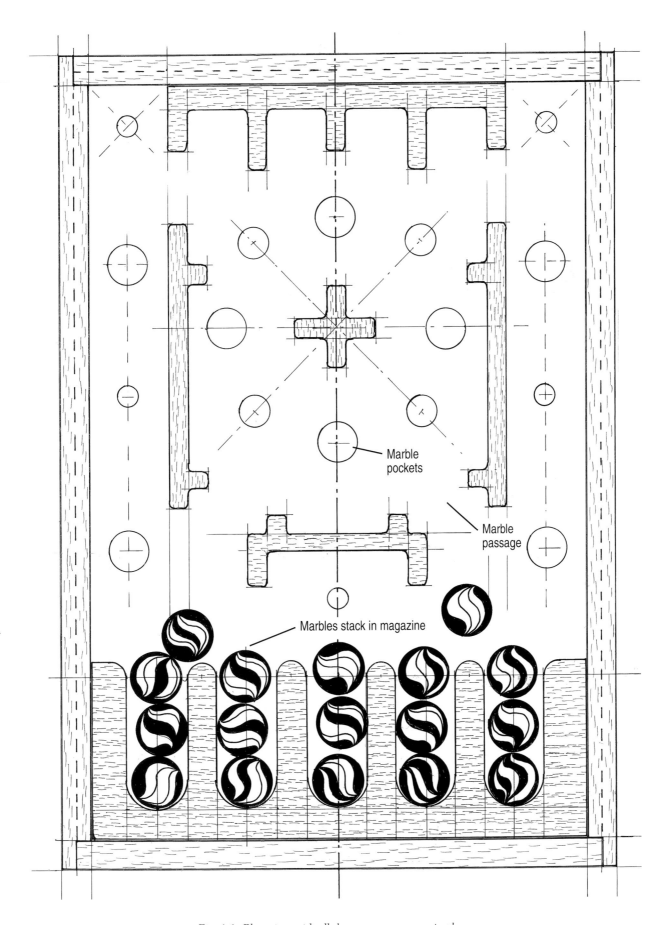

Marble
pockets

Marble
passage

Marbles stack in magazine

Fig. 1-1. Plan view with all the component parts in place.

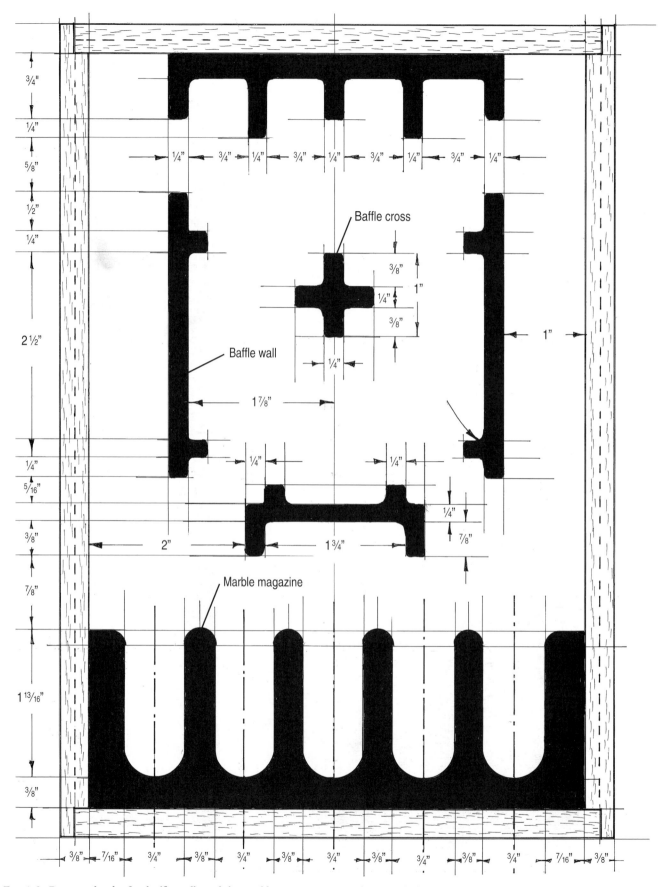

Fig. 1-2. Patterns for the five baffle walls and the marble magazine. Note the critical placing of the four main walls so that there is an easy passage for the marbles at the corners.

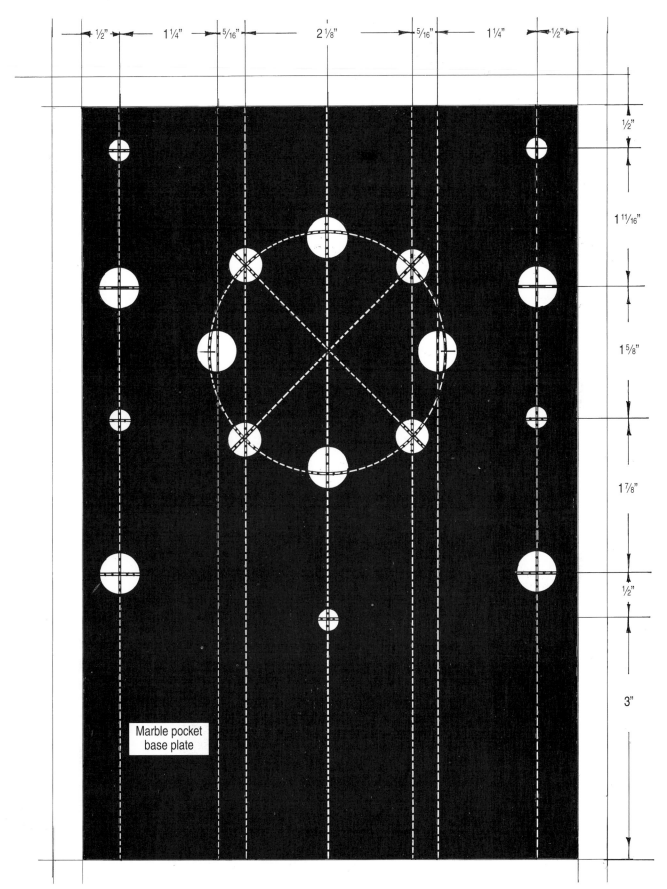

Fig. 1-3. Pattern for the marble pocket base plate. Though the figure shows three different sizes for the pocket holes, you could make the game even more difficult by having all the holes small.

Fig. 1-4. *Cutting the baffle walls on the scroll saw. It's easy enough, as long as you hold the workpiece firmly down, make sure that the saw table is polished, and see to it that the blade is well tensioned.*

to a thickness of ¼ inch, and sand or scrape it to a smooth finish.

2. Study the working drawings, take note of the way all the angles are smoothed out with hand-drawn radius curves, and then use a pencil, rule, and square to draw the design of the baffles on the best face of the wood.

3. Shade in the waste side of the line. Make sure the baffles are about ¼ inch wide throughout.

4. Fit the finest blade in the scroll saw, and adjust the tension so that the blade pings when plucked. Feed the workpiece into the saw at a steady, controlled pace (see Fig. 1-4).

5. When you have achieved the five baffles, rub the edges down to a good finish with a scrap of fine-grade sandpaper.

Making the Marble Magazine

1. Take the wood that you have selected for the marble magazine, plane it to a thickness of a little over 1¼ inches, and then scrape it to a good finish. Make sure that the wood is square, with true faces and edges.

2. Noting that the grain needs to run across the width of the box, use a pencil, rule, square, and compass to mark the design of the magazine on the best face of the wood. Shade in the areas of waste so that the line of cut is clearly defined, and prick in the center points at the bottom of the marble chambers.

3. When you are happy with the way the design is laid out, fit a ¾-inch-diameter Forstner bit in the drill, and start by running a hole through the bottom of each of the marble chambers (see Fig. 1-5).

4. Move to the band saw and run cuts to the waste side of the drawn lines and into the holes. Go easily, being careful not to split the relatively fragile short grain (see Fig. 1-6).

Special Tip

If you are going to do a lot of small-scale woodworking that needs to have shallow, precise, smooth-sided holes or large-diameter holes, get a bench drill and a set of forstner bits. Although the Forstner bits are expensive, they do the job perfectly every time, and they last forever.

Fig. 1-5. *Run the drill bit in and out as the hole deepens, to clear the waste and to give the bit a chance to cool down.*

Fig. 1-6. Make sure that the line of cut is to the waste side of the drawn line so that the cut smoothly enters the drilled hole.

Fig. 1-7. Support the workpiece on a piece of waste wood so as to avoid damage when the point of the bit breaks through.

Drilling the Base Plate

1. Cut the board to size, and make sure that it's a crisp and clean drop-in fit in the box. Then take a pencil, rule, compass, and square, and carefully draw out the position of the holes, taking note of the three different diameter sizes. Mark the center point with an awl.

2. Secure the thin plywood on a stout piece of board, and then run the holes through on the drill (see Fig. 1-7). Go at it very slowly, so that the drill exits cleanly.

3. Wipe around the inside of the holes with a scrap of fine-grade sandpaper.

Assembly

1. When you have achieved all seven component parts—the base plate board, the five baffles, and the marble magazine—clear away all the dust and debris and test-fit the base board and marble magazine. If necessary, trim back to a good fit. Familiarize yourself with the placement of the various pieces (see Fig. 1-8).

2. Smear a small amount of PVA glue on the underside of the base plate, well away from the drilled holes and the edges, then set it down in position in the box. Press it firmly in place.

3. Dab a small amount of PVA glue on the underside and edges of the marble magazine and the baffles, and set them in place.

4. If all is correct, the top face of the magazine will be slightly lower than the underside of the top slot (see Fig. 1-9).

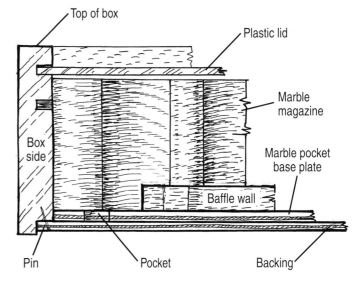

Fig. 1-8. The top face of the marble magazine needs to be slightly lower than the top slot so there is room for the plastic sheet to slide in place.

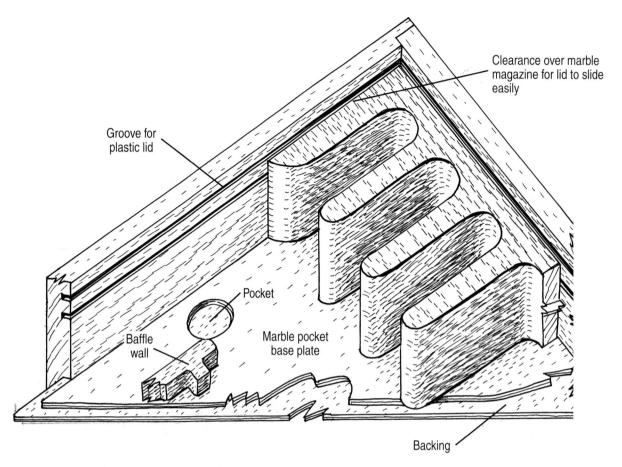

Groove for
plastic lid

Clearance over marble
magazine for lid to slide
easily

Pocket

Baffle
wall

Marble pocket
base plate

Backing

Fig. 1-9. The component parts need to be a tight push fit, but not so tight that you put a strain on the box.

5. Wipe the whole works over with beeswax, and burnish the surface to a good finish. Finally, slide the clear plastic sheet in place and fix it with a brass nail, as described in the section on Making the Basic Box.

Afterthoughts and Troubleshooting

• The choice of wood is important, as it's much easier to make successful cuts on a scroll saw if the wood is hard and free from knots. You also don't want to use a large, open-grained wood like English oak or a loose-grained wood like jelutong. The joy of using a wood like American cherry is that it leaves the scroll saw with the sawn face so smooth that it requires only a minimum of sanding or scraping.

• Though Forstner drill bits cut beautiful holes, you have to be careful when drilling deep, large-diameter holes in hardwood that you don't push them too hard and cause overheating. Repeatedly run the bit in and out to clear the waste and allow the bit time to cool down.

• Always do a trial fitting before gluing. Beginners often become impatient and apply all the glue, only to then find that a part doesn't fit.

Project 2

Marble Deceleration Honeycomb Maze

Little cells and modules, such as those seen in architectural drawings, beehives, Japanese screens, Chinese puzzles, and mazes, are fascinating. There is something beautiful about the perfect repetition and the way one little unit relates to another. And so it is with this project—there is something really exciting about the way the strips of wood slot together and all add up to make the grid of cells. And once you pierce selected cells with drilled holes, then the whole thing becomes intriguing and Kafkaesque.

The object of the game is get the marble—we used a ball bearing—from one corner of the box through to the other. It looks pretty easy, doesn't it? Well, of course it is . . . you only have to tip and nudge the box so that the ball bearing runs from one cell to another, using your vast intellect to figure out the route. It's easy—so long as you can avoid the marbles trapped in cells and running into dead ends, and you don't tip the box too far so that the ball bearing zooms through a whole series of cells.

Design, Structure, and Techniques

There are any number of exciting possibilities with a maze game of this character. The drilled holes can be different sizes, the holes can lead through to dead-end zones, you can top off some of the cells so that there are blind areas, or marbles can be trapped in cells. The best way to design the maze is to draw grids out on paper and try out various convoluted routes, traps, and dead ends. The smaller the scale, the smaller the marbles, and the greater the number of cells, the more of a challenge it all becomes. If you use very thin strips of ⅛ inch thick, a small ball bearing of about ⅛ inch diameter, and cells of about ¼ inch square, you'll have a maze of beautiful complexity.

Perhaps the biggest challenge with this particular game is in the making. It's not so much that any single task is particularly tricky—measuring out, cutting the slots, and drilling the holes are all relatively easy—but the project calls for a fair amount of patient measuring and a deft touch. When you are drilling the holes, for example, the wood between the holes and the slots is so short grained and fragile that you have to be careful not to force the pace and split the wood. If you have doubts about your tools or your skills, make a trial run with strips of scrap wood and see how it goes. As for putting the maze together, the good news is that once the strips of wood are slotted together, the whole structure begins to become stronger.

This project needs to be worked with pretty specific tools. Among other tools, we used a cabinet scraper to skim the strips to a good finish, a band saw with a fine blade to make cuts on either side of the slots, a ¼-inch-wide chisel to pare out the slot waste, and a ½-inch-diameter Forstner bit for the holes.

The primary challenge here is being able to cut the slots so that one strip is a nice push fit within another. And you do have to carefully plan out the sequence of holes so that there is only one route home. There also need to be a good number of dead-end routes. Draw out clear designs on paper, decide which option you want to go for, and then number and letter the strips as shown in the working drawings to avoid mistakes (see Figs. 2-1, 2-2, and 2-3).

Choosing the Wood

For this project, the wood must be strong along the run of the grain, free from knots, and reasonably tight textured. As our box was made from brown oak, we

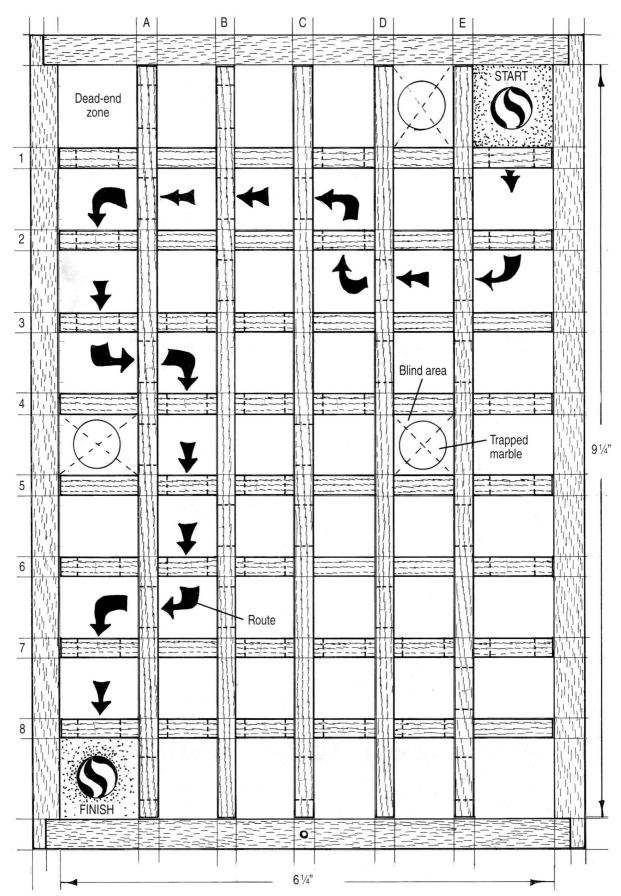

Fig. 2-1. Plan view with all the component parts in place. Note the route shown by the arrows, plus the dotted lines that indicate the various dead end routes.

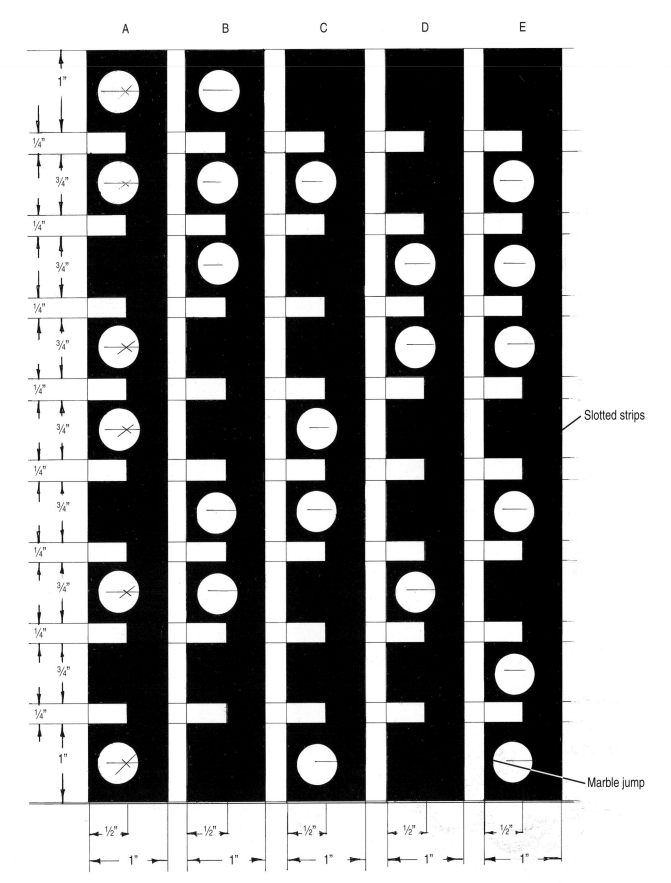

Fig. 2-2. Patterns for the long strips, showing all the slots and holes. Note how the holes need to be set nearer to the bottom of the strip than to the top.

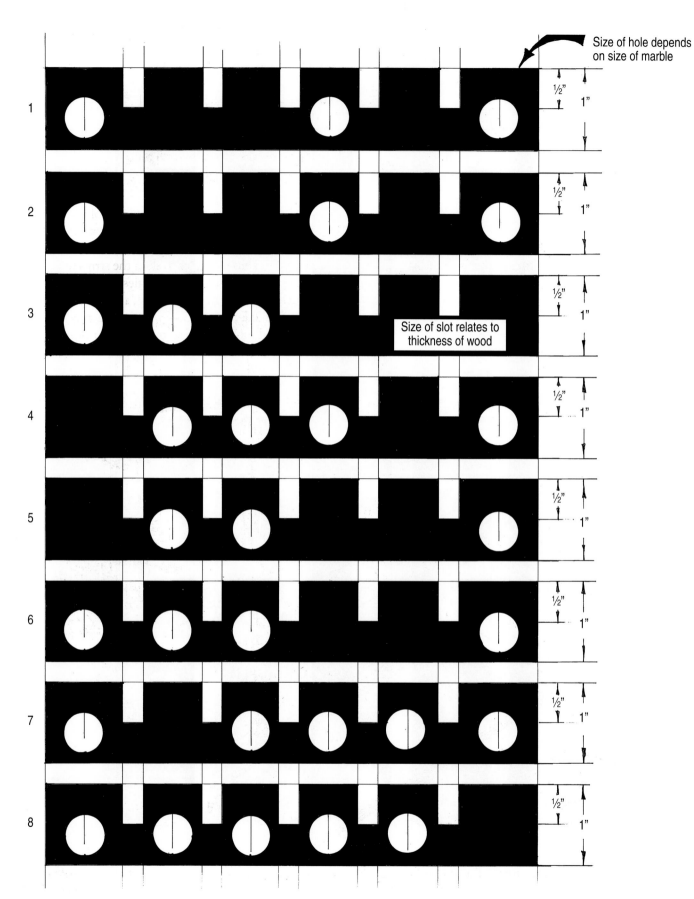

Size of hole depends
on size of marble

1   ½"   1"

2   ½"   1"

3   Size of slot relates to
    thickness of wood
    ½"   1"

4   ½"   1"

5   ½"   1"

6   ½"   1"

7   ½"   1"

8   ½"   1"

Fig. 2-3. Patterns for the short strips, with all the slots and holes in place.

chose contrasting, light-colored wood for the strips. We used ¼-inch-thick-by-1-inch-wide strips of English larch, a species of pine, but you could also use white pine, ash, beech, or just about any straight-grained wood you like. If you prefer something fancier, you could have light strips running one way and dark strips the other, or you could have alternating light and dark strips in both directions. There are lots of exciting pattern options.

Making the Project
Preparing the Strips
1.   When you have studied the project picture (see color section) and the working drawings (see Figs. 2-1, 2-2, and 2-3), take your chosen wood and give it one more good, long lookover to make sure that it is free from splits.

2.   Plane the wood down to a thickness of just over ¼ inch, saw it into strips a little wider than 1 inch, and then saw it slightly longer than the inside box size, so that you have a small amount of cutting waste to play with. Go for five long strips at 10 inches and eight strips at 7 inches.

3.   Build two simple stop jigs, one to hold the strips flat down and singly (see Fig. 2-4), and another to hold them on edge and in batches.

4.   Use the cabinet scraper to skim the strips to a good finish. Experiment with various angles to the run of the grain until you achieve an efficient, shearing cut. First bring the face sides to a good finish, and then grip them on edge and in batches, and skim them all at one time to an identical width (see Fig. 2-5).

Cutting the Slots
1.   When you have achieved all thirteen strips—five long and eight short—then take the square, rule, and

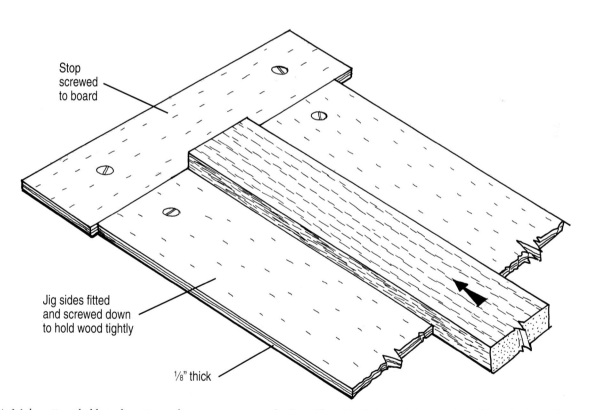

Stop screwed to board

Jig sides fitted and screwed down to hold wood tightly

⅛" thick

Fig. 2-4. Make a jig to hold single strips so that you can scrape the face sides. My jig is made from strips of ⅛-inch plywood screwed to a baseboard. In use, the workpiece is pushed into the jig so that it is nicely contained, and then worked in the direction of the arrow as shown.

Fig. 2-5. Set the batch of strips in the jig so that the grain of all the strips is running in the same direction, and work the edges with a cabinet scraper. Work one side, and then turn the batch over and work the other side.

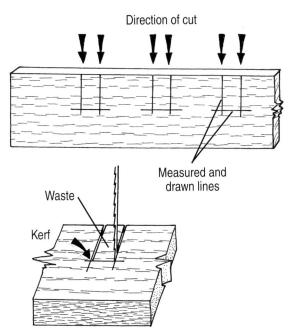

Fig. 2-6. Use a rule and square to lay out the position of the slots. Make sure that the saw kerf occurs to the waste side of the drawn lines.

knife, and very carefully lay out the position of the step-offs that go to make up the design. Note that though for the most part the step-offs go ¾ inch, ¼ inch, ¾ inch, and so on, the sequence always starts and finishes with a step-off of 1 inch (see Figs. 2-1, 2-2, and 2-3).

2. Make sure when drawing in the slots that they measure ¼ inch wide and just a tad over ½ inch deep.

3. When you are happy with the way the strips have been laid out, and when you have double-checked that all is correct, shade in the areas of waste.

4. Take the strips to the band saw—or you might use a small, fine-toothed backsaw—and run a cut at either side of the waste. It's important that the cuts be worked to the waste side of the drawn lines (see Fig. 2-6).

5. Finally, support the workpiece on the bench, then take your razor-sharp paring chisel and clear the waste (see Fig. 2-7). The best procedure is to first chop out to within about 1/16 inch of the line, and then carefully pare back to a perfect fit.

Drilling the Holes

1. First, take a good, long look at the working drawings and note that there is a short-grained weak area between the cut slots and the holes. All this means, in effect, is that you have to go nice and easy from now on—no rough handling or forcing the pace of the drill.

Fig. 2-7. First use a single chop to remove the bulk of the waste, and then carefully pare back to the mark.

2. Use the square, rule, and pencil to fix the position of the holes. The centers need to be fixed about ⅜ inch in from each slot and about ⅜ inch up from the bottom edge of the strip. Note that the short strips have the slots coming in from the top edge, whereas the long strips have the slots coming in from the bottom edge. It's very easy to goof up at this stage, so spend time getting it right. It's a good idea to pencil-label the bottom edges.

3. When you have marked all the center points, set the strips one at a time in a jig, and run the holes through on the drill (see Fig. 2-8). Have a strip of waste between the workpiece and the jig, and go slowly. Be warned—if you try to force the pace of the drill, you risk splitting the wood or creating a ragged exit hole.

4. With all the slots and holes in place, tidy up with a scrap of fine-grade sandpaper.

Assembly

1. Now it's time for a trial fitting. Go at it gently, all the while making sure that you don't put undue pressure on the area around the holes—no bending or twisting. You shouldn't need to use brute force. If any part threatens to stick, very carefully ease the whole works apart and sand back the offending edge. Work systematically from one side across to the other (see Fig. 2-9).

Special Tip

It helps at this stage, when the strips are put together dry, if the wood is first rubbed down with beeswax. At this point, you don't have to worry about getting wax on a part that is to be glued. You will find that the wax eases the friction on tight-fitting areas.

---

2. When you have achieved a good fit of all the strips, align the grid on top of the box and use a knife to mark in the lengths of the strips. Aim for a good push fit, neither too tight nor too loose.

3. Ease the grid apart. Mark the ends of the strips off with a square, and then use the bench hook and a fine-bladed saw to cut back the waste.

4. Rub down the sawn ends, slot the strips back together (see Fig. 2-10), drop the whole works in the box, and use colored felt-tip pens to shade in the "start" and "finish" cells on diagonally opposite corners (see Fig. 2-1, 2-2, and 2-3).

5. Finally, pop the trapped marbles in place, drop in the ball bearing, slide in the clear plastic sheet, and the game is ready for playing.

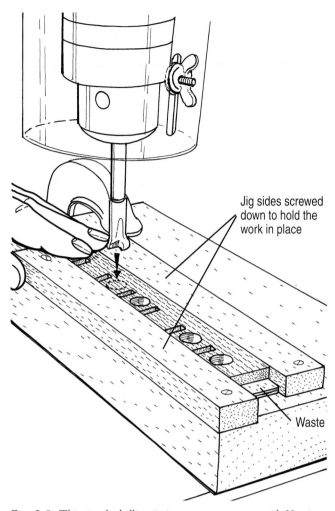

Jig sides screwed down to hold the work in place

Waste

Fig. 2-8. This simple drilling jig is great, easy-to-use aid. You just slide a strip of waste plywood in the jig, align and clamp the jig so that the hole center points are always going to be on track, and then drill the holes. The fact that the jig is clamped firmly ensures that the holes are on target.

Fig. 2-9. Fit and fiddle until it all comes together, all the while being careful that you don't use too much force.

Fig. 2-10. Don't lose patience if the last strip fails to slide neatly into place; just take note of the tight-fitting areas and rub them down some more.

Afterthoughts and Troubleshooting

• It's always a good idea when you are making multiples—especially when you have to build jigs—to make more parts than you need. For this project, make a couple trial strips from waste wood, then use your good wood to make seven long strips and ten short—two extra each way. This way, you can choose the best of the bunch for your project, and you have spares if something goes wrong.

• If you have to make small, cut-to-length multiples as in this project, it's a good idea to make yourself a sizing bench hook. This is a wide bench hook with a fixed stop at the top, as usual, and an adjustable stop to the left. In use, you measure and cut the first strip to length, then you set this length in the hook and slide the left-hand stop to butt against the end. From then on, all you do is slide the wood to be cut into the hook so that the left-hand end butts hard up against the stop, and then make a cut with the saw running against the side of the top stop.

Ultimate-Level Marble Labyrinth

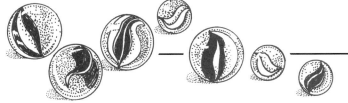

The word *labyrinth* conjures up images of deep and sinuous tunnels, passages, and catacombs. The idea of being lost in a deep, dark labyrinth is scary. There might be any number of traps, pitfalls, and hazards along the way: holes, slithery reptiles that live in the dark, cobwebs dangling from the roof. How would you get out if you couldn't see your way? Okay, so you might get occasional glimpses of light from cracks overhead, but imaging stumbling around in the dark with only your senses of touch and hearing to guide you, not knowing whether you are walking up, down, or around in circles.

This game draws its inspiration from such labyrinths. You get to see fleeting glimpses of the marble as it rolls past the holes, and you can hear the sounds the marble makes as it clunks against the sides of the labyrinth, but otherwise you are working in the dark. You can't really see the marble, and you never get to see the shape of the walls within the labyrinth. All you know for sure is that the marble goes in one hole and out the other. And even the entrance and exit holes are none too obvious. And as for the soft-touch marbles, not only are they good to touch, but better yet, they also muddy the waters when the player is trying to see what's going on.

The Marble Labyrinth is a great game to play. You simply pop the marble in the slightly larger hole at the top left, and then do your best to get it out of the large hole five rows down. Very soon your sense of hearing tunes in to tell you how far the marble has rolled. The sound the marble makes as it bumps around is quite different depending on whether it is bumping into a side or an end wall.

Design, Structure, and Techniques

Look over the project picture (see color section) and the working drawings (see Figs. 3-1 and 3-2). Apart from the box, this game is built up from easy-to-make component parts. The inside walls are made from short strips of wood that are simply butted together and glued—no joints or complex fitting. Study the drawings carefully, and note how the whole design is based on a square grid, with the cells being ¾ inch square and the walls made from ¼-inch-thick strips. This box has been reduced to a one-groove option (see the section on Making the Basic Box). The soft-touch marbles are simply marbles supported on pads of soft sponge.

As to this design, though we have gone for a relatively simple, easy-to-make option, there are any number of exciting possibilities. For example, you could use a much smaller marble and build the labyrinth on a ¼ inch grid. You could have little pitfall pockets for the marble to fall into and unseen pins and protrusions sticking out from the walls to interrupt the marble on its passage. You could make the viewing holes much smaller, or you could even do away with the viewing holes altogether and create a labyrinth that relies totally on your sense of hearing.

Choosing the Wood

Though you might use just about any wood for the inside walls—after all, they are more or less hidden from view—you do need a wood that is free from knots and splits. We simply used some oak and ash scraps. You could even use strips of waste ply or wood salvaged from packing crates. The strips need to be ¼ inch thick and about 1⅛ inches wide.

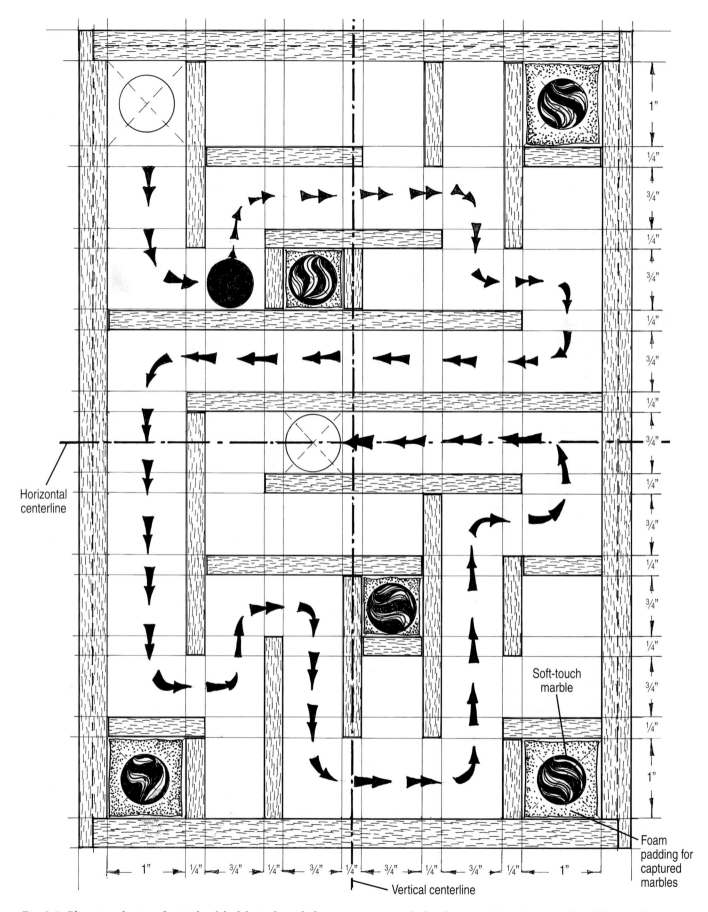

Horizontal
centerline

Soft-touch
marble

Foam
padding for
captured
marbles

Vertical centerline

1" ¼" ¾" ¼" ¾" ¼" ¾" ¼" ¾" ¼" 1"

1" ¼" ¾" ¼" ¾" ¼" ¾" ¼" ¾" ¼" 1"

Fig. 3-1. Plan view showing the inside of the labyrinth, with the escape route marked with arrows. Note the vertical and horizontal axis center lines.

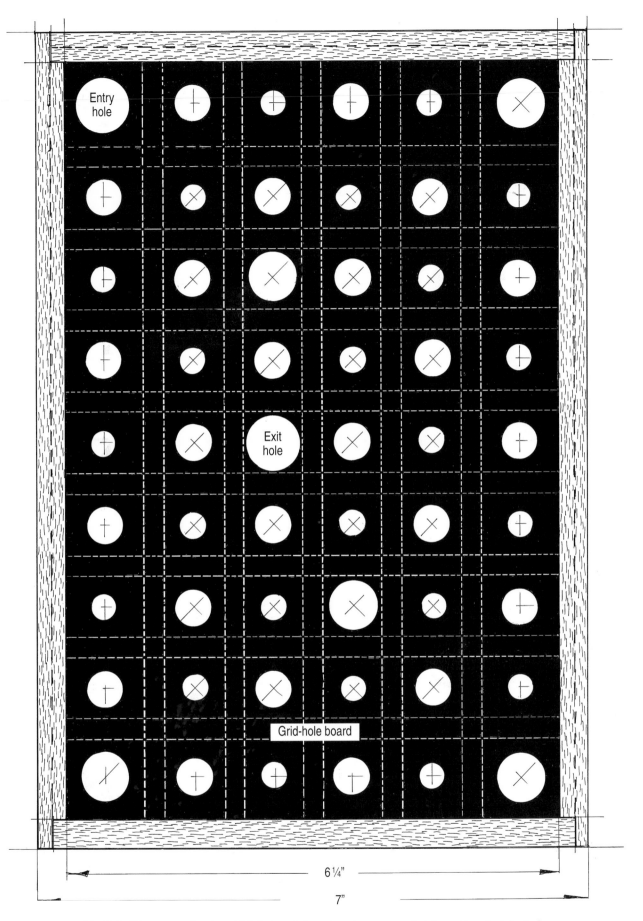

Fig. 3-2. The pattern for the grid-hole board, based on the same underlying grid as the labyrinth.

Making the Project

Laying Out the Labyrinth

1. When you have studied the designs and generally prepared all your tools so that you are ready for action, take a sheet of tracing paper cut to the size of the box, and lay it out with a ¾-inch grid, as shown in the working drawings (see Figs. 3-1 and 3-2). If you work out from center lines, as marked in the working drawings on both the horizontal and vertical axes, the edge cells will be 1 by ¾ inch, the ones at the corners 1 by 1 inch, and all those at the center ¾ by ¾ inch.

2. Once the grid structure is drawn out, play around with various routes and options until you have one that strikes your fancy. Keep in mind that the whole object of the game is to give the player as many false leads and dead ends as possible. There are countless possible options.

3. Finalize the plan and draw in the arrows, double-check that the poor old player will eventually find a route through, then shade in the pattern of walls on the tracing, and pencil-press the design through to the plywood base board (see Fig. 3-3).

4. Glue and nail the base into the box.

Cutting and Fitting the Strips

1. Though the strips are simply cut to length, glued in place, and then more or less hidden from view, this is not to say that you should settle for a mess of splinters. To my way of thinking, this is a great time to perfect your sawing and planing techniques. Start by planing the wood to a thickness of ¼ inch. The best procedure is to use a smoothing plane and to set the bench up with a simple pattern of stops. All you do is set the sawn board flat down on the bench, nail a few strips of ⅛-inch ply to the far end and the sides to hold the workpiece in place, and to go work (see Fig. 3-4).

Fig. 3-3. Use the square to make sure that the grid lines are true.

2. When you have achieved a good amount of ¼-inch thick stuff, planed and faced on both sides, take a metal straightedge and a knife and lay it out into 1¼-inch-wide strips.

3. Use a ripsaw to cut the wood down, and then plane the edges of the strips down to a good finish. Aim to skim about ⅟₁₆ inch from each edge so that you end up with a finished size of 1⅛ inches.

4. Transfer the measurements from the working drawing, and cut the strip wood into the appropriate lengths. Use a block plane to bring all the sawn ends to a smooth, true finish.

5. When all the pieces that go to make up the design are cut to size, pencil-label the bottom edges and mating faces.

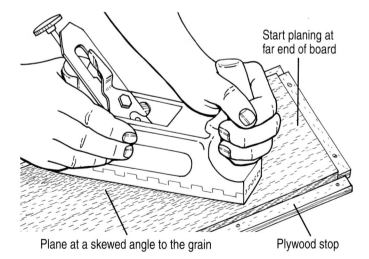

Start planing at far end of board

Plane at a skewed angle to the grain

Plywood stop

Fig. 3-4. With the board held secure by the plywood stops, take the smoothing plane, make sure that the cutting iron is razor sharp and set for the finest of cuts, and then work with an angled shearing action.

6. One piece at a time, take the strips, smear glue on the bottom edge and mating faces, and carefully set them in place in the box. Spend time making sure they are well placed in relation to one another and at right angles to the base (see Fig. 3-5).

Drilling and Fitting the Grid-Hole Board

1. Cut and fit the grid-hole board, as described in the section on Making the Basic Box, make sure that it is a nice push fit in the top groove, and then draw out the basic grid as shown in the working drawings (see Figs. 3-1 and 3-2).

2. With a rule and pencil, mark the center point of each cell by drawing crossed diagonals.

3. Once all the center points are in place, make decisions as to the sizes of the various holes. The entrance and exit holes have to be big enough to allow for easy passage, and the holes for all the other cells must be smaller than the diameter of the marble, but there's no saying that you can't go for very small sizes for the glimpsing holes. We used ¼-inch and ⅜-inch glimpsing holes, ⅝-inch entrance and exit holes, and ⅝-inch captive marble holes. Note that we use large-size marbles for the captive cells.

4. When you have decided on the hole sizes, use a pillar drill to run them through. Avoid drill exit damage by having the workpiece supported on a piece of waste

Fig. 3-5. Glue and position the individual strips, making sure that they are carefully aligned with the underlying grid.

wood (see Fig. 3-6). Move the waste piece after every drilling to avoid running a hole through the same spot.

5. Rub the whole works down with a fine-grade sandpaper, give it a color wash—either watercolor or alcohol—rub it down some more to remove the nubs of grain, and wax it to a dull sheen finish.

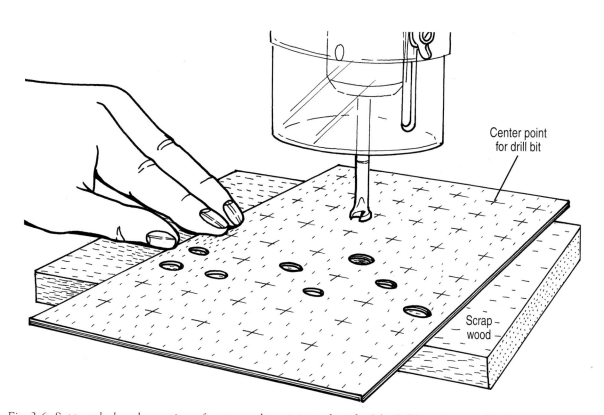

Fig. 3-6. Support the board on a piece of scrap wood to minimize the risk of the drill bit splintering the plywood as it exits.

Fig. 3-7. Pack the captive cells with layers of foam, until the marble is pushed up higher than the level of the groove.

Fig. 3-8. Carefully nudge the captive marbles down so that the grid-hole board has a clear passage to slide along its groove.

Fitting the Captive Marbles

1. Obtain some small pieces of upholstery foam big enough to fit the captive marble cells, and trim them to size. What you are after is just enough "spring" to push the marble hard into the grid-hole board, so that the marbles are held against the underside of the holes (see Fig. 3-7). Spend some time experimenting with various depths of foam.

2. When you've got it right, sit the captive marbles in their little nests of foam, and carefully slide the grid-hole board into place (see Fig. 3-8).

3. Finally, drop the labyrinth marble in the entrance hole, and the game is ready for playing.

Afterthoughts and Troubleshooting

• If you want to make this game more visually exciting, you could cover the grid-hole board with a decorative veneer. This would need to be done before the holes are drilled. Or you could go for an ebonized effect by blacking it with a felt-tip pen and burnishing it with beeswax.

• If you want a more challenging labyrinth, you could reduce the size of the cells and have two marbles, only one being small enough to exit. The idea is that the large marble would generally block the way and be a nuisance.

• You could increase the skill level by lining the labyrinth with different fabrics, such as silk, velvet, plastic, and so forth. The different textures and surfaces would confuse the issue by changing the sound as the marble rolls around.

• If you want to go for the ultimate-level game, you could have two layers of cells so that the marble can drop down into a deeper level.

Project 4

Marble-Bearing Random Number Selector

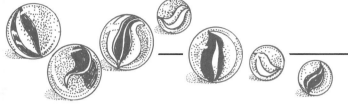

A good part of the joy, pleasure, and fascination of this project has to do with the making. It's a fun project to play with, spinning the arrow pointer and trying to guess where it's going to point next, but more than that, the actual designing and building are truly exciting and intriguing—if, that is, you enjoy working on the lathe. Though wood turning is always a uniquely gratifying woodworking activity, turning the marble bearing for this project is a skill-stretching challenge that calls for a lot of concentration and careful measuring. So if you are looking for a wood-turning challenge, this may be the project for you.

Design, Structure, and Techniques

Before jumping into this project, be aware that you'll need the use of a lathe to turn the two rings that form the bearing case. If you are eager to make this project but don't have a lathe, you can try using a scroll saw and a spoon-bit carving gouge. Cut the rings out on the scroll saw, and use the gouge to carve the semicircular grooves for the marbles. It won't be easy, but you'll get the job done. If you have any doubts about the order of work or your skill level, make a number of trial runs to work out the bugs before tackling the actual project.

Look over the working drawings (see Figs. 4-1, 4-2, and 4-3). Apart from the box, this project is made from eight primary components: an oblong dial, three roller dowels that run across the width of the box, two rings that go to make up the bearing race, an arrow pointer, and a central mushroom-headed boss.

We more or less copied the shape and form of the dial from an Arts and Crafts style clock. If you study the drawings, you will see that the positions of twelve dial marbles are achieved by dividing the underlying circle into twelve equal 30-degree segments, just like a clock, and then extending the resultant lines so that they cross the centerlines of the dial. The center points are fixed where the angle and centerlines intersect. Note that though we have popped a marble in each of the dial holes, you would use colors, numerals, letters, dots like a dice—whatever suits your fancy.

The two rings that go to make the ball race are simply two rings turned from the same disk, with the outside edge of the small inner ring and the inside edge of the large outer ring being turned with a semicircular channel. The trick is in being able to hold the disk in the lathe while at the same time being able to judge and turn the semicircular channels to match up with the diameter of your chosen race marbles. As the photographs show, it's much easier if you use a four-jaw chuck to hold the workpiece.

Marbles often tend to be imperfect, and it's important that you do your best to choose a well-matched set. If one looks a bit lopsided, is chipped, or has a slightly different diameter, look for another one.

Warning: Wood turning is always a potentially dangerous activity. You never know whether the workpiece might spin off the lathe. For safety, it's best to always wear a full-face respirator when working on the lathe; the filter prevents you from breathing the dust, and the plastic visor protects your face. If you don't have a respirator, wear safety glasses and a rubber filter-type mask.

Choosing the Wood

For this project, it's important to use a good, solid, dense-grained wood. Ideally, you should use a single slab of wood for the dial, and then use the piece cut from the center for turning the dial. That said, we used

35

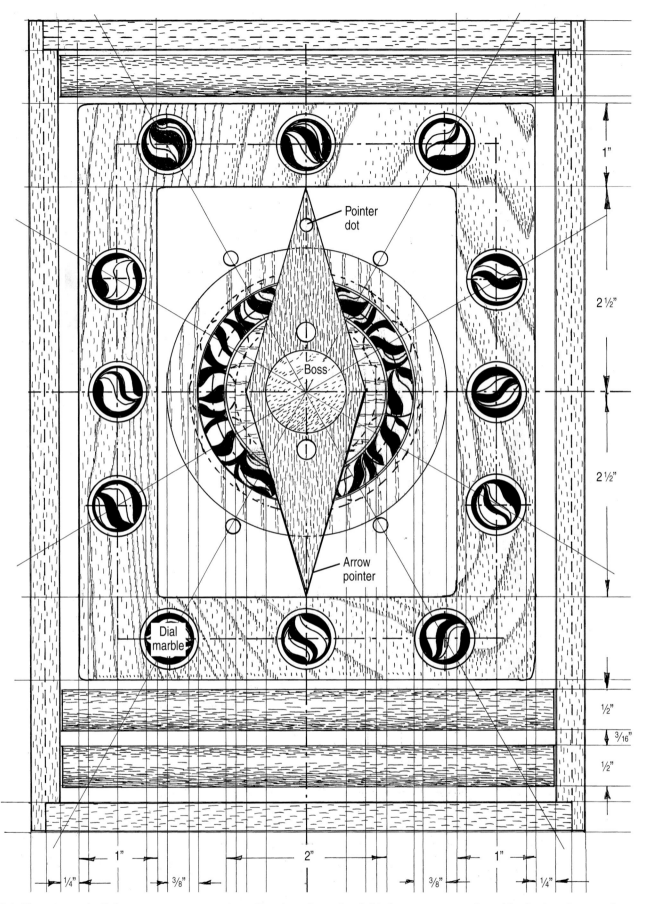

Fig. 4-1. Plan view with all the component parts in place. Note how the twelve dial hole positions are achieved by dividing the central circle into twelve equal 30-degree segments.

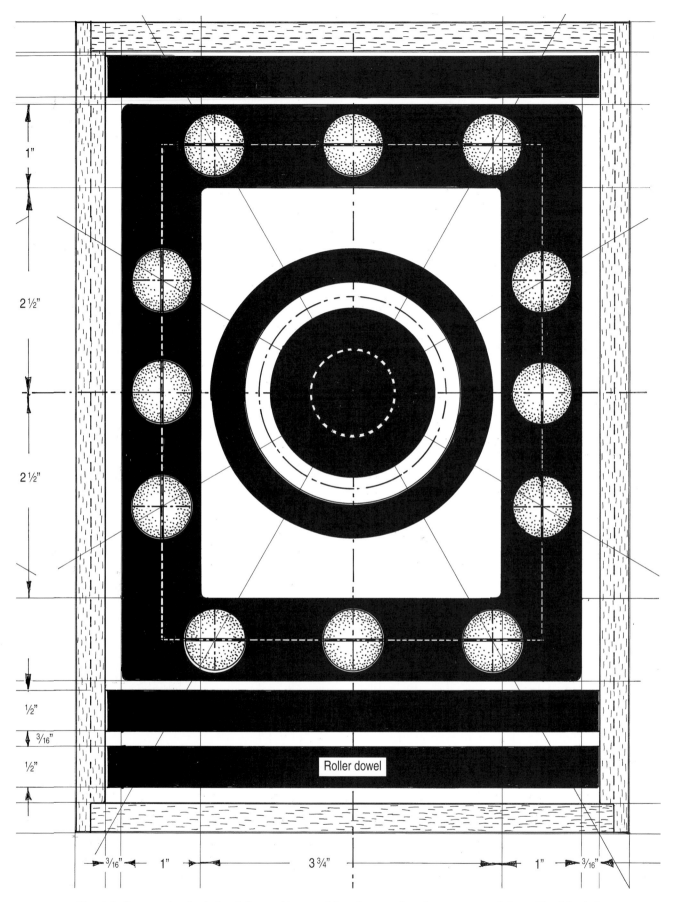

1"

2½"

2½"

½"

3/16"

½"

3/16"　1"　3¾"　1"　3/16"

Roller dowel

Fig. 4-2. Patterns for the dial and the marble race. Note the centerline that runs around the width of the dial.

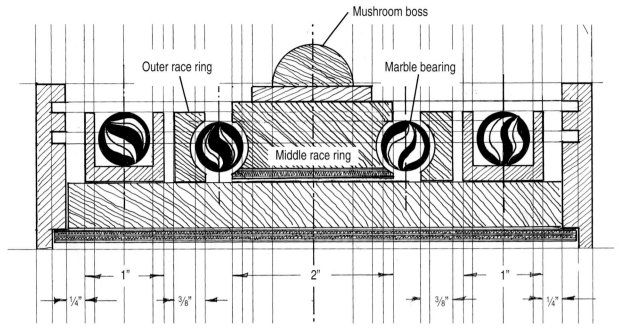

Fig. 4-3. Cross section through finished dial holes and boss showing the marbles between the race rings.

a knotty piece for the dial, with the knot cut away as waste, and a small scrap for the disk. We used ¾-inch-thick English cherry for the dial and the ring turnings, a piece of ½-inch-thick sycamore for the inside-box slab, a length of 1¼-inch-square-section beech for the boss, shop-bought dowels for the rollers, and a scrap of mahogany for the arrow.

Making the Project
Making the Dial

1. Study the working drawings (see Figs. 4-1, 4-2, and 4-3) so that you have a good, clear understanding of what goes where and how. Once you've made a box (see Making a Basic Box section) and nailed the base in position, start off by cutting the slab of 1½-inch-thick wood to size and dropping it into the box.

2. Take the slab of ¾-inch-thick wood that you've chosen for the dial, and plane it to a good finish on both sides. Fix the center point by drawing crossed diagonals, and draw in the shape of the 1-inch-wide frame that goes to make the rectangular dial. Divide the circle into twelve 30-degree segments, and extend the lines and fix the position of the holes on the dial.

3. Run a pilot hole through some part of the central waste, and then fret the form out on a scroll saw (see Fig. 4-4). The figure shows the back of the slab so that you can see how we worked around the knot. If you are using a sound slab of wood, you could use the central piece for turning the rings.

4. Having established the position of the twelve dial holes, fit the ¾-inch Forstner bit in the drill, set the depth stop on the drill so that all the holes will be the same depth, and then drill the holes to a depth of ½ inch (see Fig. 4-5).

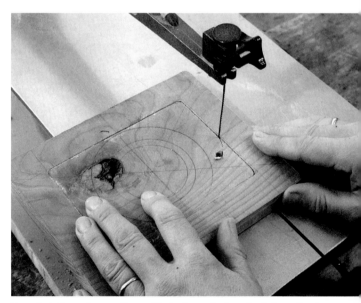

Fig. 4-4. Pass the scroll saw blade through the pilot hole, rehitch and retension the blade, and then run the line of cut to the waste side of the drawn lines. Note how we have managed to cut the dial from a piece of flawed wood, placing the knot in the central area of waste.

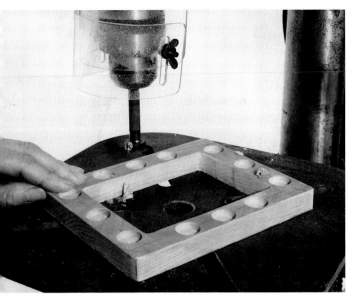

Fig. 4-5. Run all the dial holes in to an identical depth. You can't beat a forstner bit if you want to drill smooth-sided blind-bottom holes.

Turning the Ball-Race Rings

1. Use the compass to draw the 3¾-inch-diameter blank (see Fig. 4-6) and then draw in the various circles that go to make up the design of the race.

2. Cut the blank out on the band saw, run a ¼-inch-diameter hole through its thickness, and mount it in the four-jaw lathe chuck so that a little less than half its thickness is secured within the jaws of the chuck. Turn it down to a true disk at 3½ inches in diameter. Pencil-label this side of the blank "back."

Special Tip

Using a four-jaw chuck is not difficult, but depending on your chuck, you might have to place a piece of waste wood against the back of the workpiece to prevent the tool from coming into contact with the chuck.

---

3. Establish the width of the outer ring at ⅜ inch and the width of the marble race where it breaks through the surface of the disk at ⁵⁄₁₆ inch. This done, take the ¼-inch-wide parting tool and sink the band of waste so that the center of the disk falls away (see Fig. 4-7). Go at it slowly, all the while being ready to catch the center as it falls free.

4. With the outer race still in place in the chuck, take a round-nosed scraper and sink a small, semicircular channel on the inside edge of the race. Go at it cautiously, all the while along the way refitting the

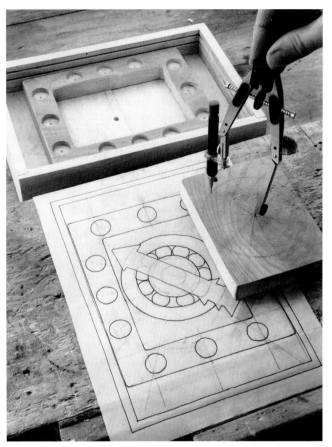

Fig. 4-6. Use a compass to draw the circles that go to make up the design of the marble race.

Fig. 4-7. Run the parting tool straight through the thickness of the wood so that the central area falls free. Go at it very gently to avoid splitting the wood.

Fig. 4-8. *Cut the semicircular groove in the inside of the large wheel. Use the central area to help judge the depth of the groove.*

inner circle so as to be able to judge just how deep the semicircular channel needs to be (see Fig. 4-8).

5. When you are happy with the outer part of the race, turn it around in the chuck and turn the other half of its thickness down to a true diameter of 3½ inches.

6. Fit the inner disk in the chuck, and turn a semicircular groove around its outer edge in much the same way as already described. Look at the working drawing cross section (see Fig. 4-3), and note how the depth of the semicircular groove needs to be worked so that the marbles are a contained loose fit.

Putting the Ball Race Together

1. Set the outer race ring in place in the box, and mark around it with a pencil. Drill four ¼-inch-diameter holes in the base slab at 1, 5, 7, and 11 o'clock, and glue stubs of dowel in place in the holes so that the outer ring of the race is held in place.

2. Hold the two parts of the race so that the back is facing you, and then carefully ease the marbles in place (see Fig. 4-9). This stage isn't easy; the marbles will keep popping out, and you might well have to rework

one or another of the component parts to fit, so be patient.

3. When you have achieved a good spinning fit, cut a small disk of ⅛-inch-thick plywood, and glue and nail it to the back face of the central part of the race (see Fig. 4-10).

4. All the marbles should be nicely captured, and the two parts of the race should be held one within another, in such a way that when the bearing is put with the back face down on a flat surface, the plywood disk is free to move.

Fig. 4-9. *One at a time, carefully ease the marbles in place between the two turnings that go to make up the bearing. If the bearing sticks fast when you have more than half the number of marbles in place, you will have to put one or another of the turnings back on the lathe and slightly deepen the semicircular groove.*

Fig. 4-10. *Cut a disk of ⅛-inch-thick plywood, chamfer the edge, and glue and nail it on the back of the central disk. Once this disk is in position, the two turned components are held in place.*

Fig. 4-11. Once you are happy with the shape of the mushroom, use the point of a skew chisel to remove the small piece of tailstock waste.

Fig. 4-12. Build a jig around the workpiece to hold it securely, and then plane it on both sides down to the required 3/16-inch thickness.

Turning the Mushroom Boss Knob

1. After again studying the working drawing, take your chosen piece of 1¼-inch-square-section wood and mount it on the lathe between centers.

2. Use the rule and dividers to lay out all the step-offs that go to make up the design. Starting from the tailstock end, allow ½ inch for tailstock waste, ½ inch for the mushroom, and about ¾ inch for the stem, and the rest for headstock chuck waste.

3. Use the parting tool to sink the tailstock waste and to reduce the diameter of the stem to about ½ inch.

4. Use the skew chisel to turn the shape of the mushroom head. Aim for a half-sphere form with a radius of ½ inch (see Fig. 4-11).

Planing and Shaping the Arrow Pointer

1. The problem here is not so much how to shape the arrow—that's easy enough—but rather, how to hold the wood while you're planing it down to such a thinness. The trick is to make a little planing jig. Set the wood down on the bench and hold it in place with strips of ⅛-inch-thick plywood. Butt the plywood hard up against the workpiece and secure it with panel nails, with the heads of the nails being punched below the surface.

2. Set the wood in the jig. Plane it to a good finish on one side, then flip it over and plane it down to a finished thickness of 3/16 inch (see Fig. 4-12).

3. Take the 3/16-inch-thick piece of wood at 1½ inches wide and 5 inches long, draw crossed diagonals to mark the center point, and then draw centerlines to split the

width and the length. Finally, use a fine saw and the block plane to make the arrow pointer shape.

Assembly and Finishing

1. When you have achieved all the component parts, then comes the exciting task of putting it together. Start by gluing the baseboard in the box.

2. Glue the three roller dowels in place, glue the marble race in the center, and then glue the dial in position (see Fig. 4-13). *Note:* When you're gluing the

Fig. 4-13. Make sure that all the component parts are well centered and aligned, then glue them in place.

Fig. 4-14. Finish up by drilling four ¼-inch-diameter holes through the arrow pointer: one for the center fixing, one for the decorative dot to indicate the point of the arrow, and two for the dowel stub fixings.

marble race, put glue on the outer ring only, so that the center is free to turn.

3. Glue the arrow pointer on the center of the race, glue the mushroom boss in place, and fix the arrow with a couple of additional dowel stubs (see Fig. 4-14).

4. Finally, glue the marbles or whatever else you've decided to use in the dial holes, give the whole works a burnishing with beeswax, and the project is finished.

Afterthoughts and Troubleshooting

• When making the marble race, keep in mind two factors: It's vital that you get a well-matched set of marbles, and the wood must be well seasoned. If you get damp, partially seasoned wood, it will continue to dry out once the race has been turned, with the effect that the race will gradually become oval in shape and cease to function.

• If the race is a little bit stiff, you can ease things by dribbling a small amount of fine oil onto the marbles.

Project 5

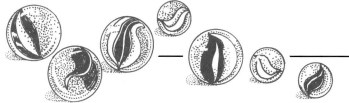

Marble Ejector

This idea came to me when I was standing in a busy airport waiting to meet my son. There I was in the after-midnight hours, hot, thirsty, and very tired, waiting and watching as hundreds of people of all shapes and sizes funneled through the narrow gate, when it came to me that perhaps it would save a lot of time and effort if we had some sort of mechanical plunger to propel people on their way. I began to picture all manner of plungers, ejectors, scoops, elevators, and moving carriageways. Swift and superefficient, maybe, and a wonderful idea for ejecting marbles, but not what you might call people friendly. As to other applications of my inspired invention, how about a machine for plunging the kids onto the school bus, or maybe a machine to help unwanted after-dinner guests on their way? There are any number of exciting possibilities.

At any rate, this project is a device designed to catch the marbles and plunge them on their way through the upper side vents. In action, with the box standing upright, you turn the handle, causing the plunger to go down, and one or more marbles roll along the side-feed channel and into the main tube. If you are lucky, when the plunger goes up, it ejects one of the marbles up through the main tube and out of one of the side exit vents. It isn't easy—the plunger has a nasty habit of getting stuck, and the marbles seem to have a mind of their own—but it is good fun.

Design, Structure, and Techniques

There are many possible variations on the basic theme. Given that there is always going to be a drive wheel with a plunger moving up and down through the main tube, there are any number of ways that you can control the flow of marbles. You can have little control gates to the side, a much larger funnel at the top, wider feed channels, and so on.

The plunger needs to be smooth curved so that it nicely deflects off the sides of the tube. If it is flat topped and sharp edged, it tends to jam tight on the upstroke. The upside-down funnel shape that leads up to the piston tube is so designed that when the plunger is on the downstroke, it is able to veer left and right to accommodate the length of the connecting rod.

Two basic construction techniques are used: wood turning and working on the scroll saw. The flywheel and the knob are turned on the lathe; all the other parts are made on the scroll saw. The only tricky thing is turning the wheel. The problem is that the front face of the wheel needs to be recessed so that its fixing pivot can be set at a low level so that it doesn't get in the way of the connecting rod. If you look at the working drawing (see Fig. 5-3), you will see in the cross section showing the wheel that whereas the rim is relatively thick, the base is thin, somewhere between $1/16$ and $1/8$ inch thick. The trick is in being able to achieve the turning without breaking through. The secret is to use a four-jaw chuck to hold the disk. It's easy if you can grip the wheel by its rim and turn it down without worrying about cutting into the screw of the screw-chuck or whatever.

For placing and fixing the component parts in the box, the best method is to use locating dowels. These enable you to experiment with various shapes and positions while everything is held firmly to the base slab. If you are having a trial fitting, it's no good if half the components are floating around loose or glued tight; they must be positively located and yet removable.

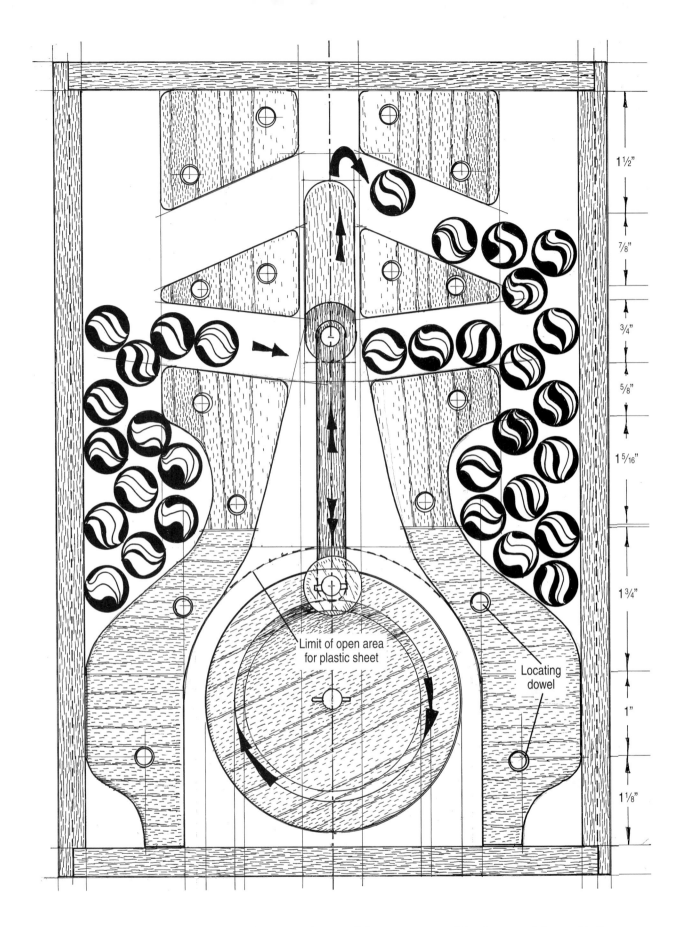

Fig. 5-1. *Plan view with all the component parts in place. Note the up-and-down movement of the plunger and the possible flow patterns of the marbles.*

1½"

⅞"

¾"

⅝"

1⁵⁄₁₆"

1¾"

1"

1⅛"

Limit of open area
for plastic sheet

Locating
dowel

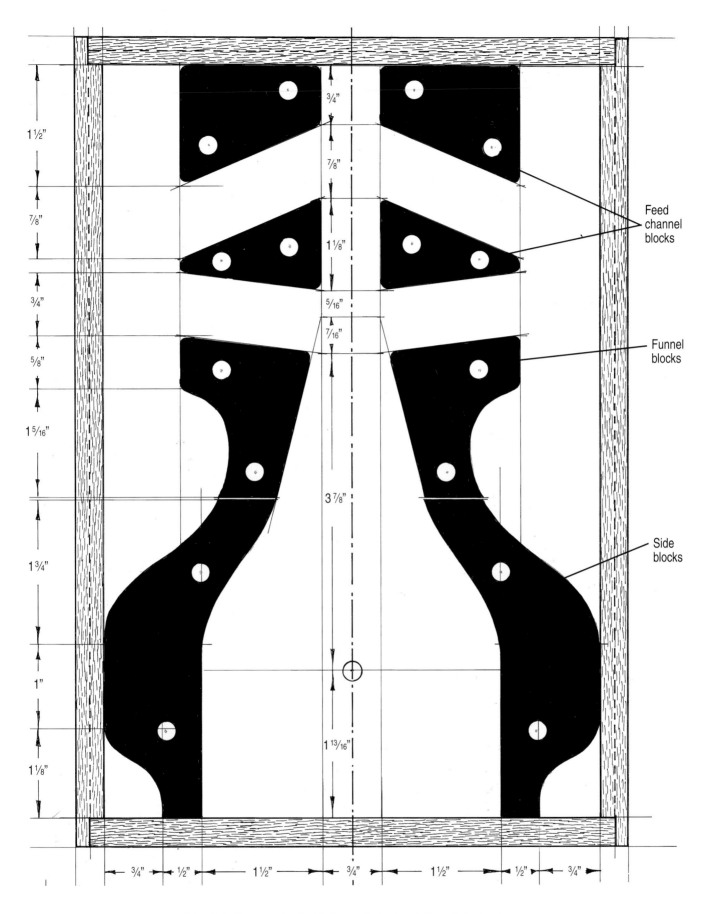

Fig. 5-2. *Patterns for the blocks, with the dowel fixing holes in place.*

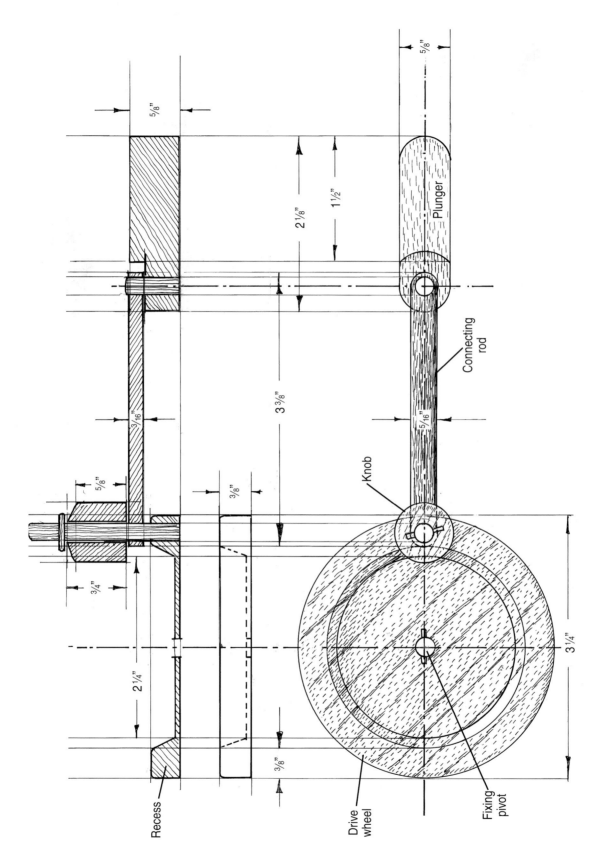

Fig. 5-3. Plan and cross-section views of the drive wheel, the turning knob, the connecting rod, and the plunger.

5/8"

1 1/2"

2 1/8"

Plunger

Connecting rod

3 3/8"

5/16"

5/8"

3/16"

Knob

3/4"

3/8"

2 1/4"

3 1/4"

Recess

Drive wheel

3/8"

Fixing pivot

Fig. 5-4. It's easier to drill the pattern of holes before you fret out the form, because you have more to hold.

Fig. 5-5. Use the drilled holes as a template pattern for the base slab holes.

Fitting the clear plastic sheet is slightly complicated, but only inasmuch as it needs to be shaped so that the whole wheel area is open, leaving the crank handle free to move. The best way of making the cut is to use the scroll saw fitted with a special blade designed to cut plastics.

There is a very fine tolerance between the plunger pivot and the plastic sheet, and the thickness of the connecting rod and the height of the wheel rim. It's best to study the working drawings and then use some scrap wood to make a full prototype before building the actual project.

Choosing the Wood
As this project has a lot of visible surfaces that are fretted into fancy shapes and then drilled, it's important to use attractive, dense-grained woods that finish well on end-grain faces. A choice wood will cut so smoothly that it doesn't need sanding, whereas a poor wood will present a rough-sawn face. Woods like cherry, plum, apple, maple, sycamore, or beech are best. Avoid loose-grained woods like jelutong or sticky woods like some species of pine. We used American cherry for the base slab, all the main cutouts, and the turnings; a scrap of plum for the connecting rod; and beech for all the dowels. You need ¾-inch-thick wood for the main cutouts, ½-inch-thick wood for the wheel, and ⅝-inch-thick wood for the base slab. Note how we have varied the run of the grain to give contrast.

Making the Project
Making the Blocks, First Fitting, and Fretting
1. Take a good, long look at the working drawings (see Figs. 5-1, 5-2, and 5-3) so that you have a completely clear understanding of what goes where and how, then spend time inspecting your chosen wood. Closely study the various pieces and make sure that they are free from splits, knots, and ragged grain. If you see the start of a split, be it ever so small, a knot in a critical area, or some other flaw, reject that piece. It's important that the wood is in good shape, so take your time.

2. When you are happy with the wood, trace the various blocks that go to make up the design, and pencil-press the images onto the best face of the wood.

3. Draw in the position of the dowel holes, and run them through with a ¼-inch-diameter Forstner bit. Have the workpiece backed with a block of waste wood to ensure that the exit holes are clean-cut (see Fig. 5-4).

4. While the scroll saw and the drill are up and running, cut and drill the disk blank that you are going to use for the turned wheel.

5. Set the blocks in place in the box, and transfer the dowel fixing holes through to the base slab.

6. Fit and fix the blocks in place in the box, and use a pencil to link up the lines of the design so that they run smoothly from one block to another (see Fig. 5-5).

7. When you are happy with the overall design, cut out the various component parts on the scroll saw (see Fig. 5-6).

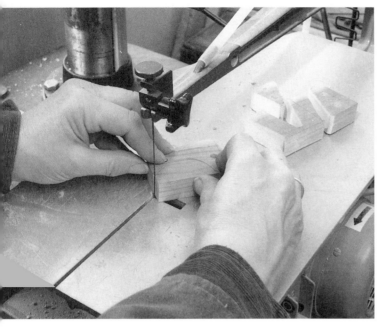

Fig. 5-6. *Use the scroll saw to fret out the shape of the blocks. If the blade is new and well tensioned, the sawn face will hardly need to be sanded.*

Making and Fitting the Plunger and Connecting Rod

1. Take a look at the working drawing cross-section details (see Fig. 5-3), and note the thickness of the two components: The plunger is ⅝ inch thick, and the connecting rod is ³/₁₆ inch. Note the way the rod is recessed into the top face of the plunger block.

2. Take the little piece of straight-grained wood you have chosen for the rod, and use a pencil, square, and rule to lay out the design. Draw in an end-to-end centerline, and establish the center points of the two holes.

3. Run the two holes through with the ¼-inch-diameter Forstner bit, and cut out the shape on the scroll saw.

4. When you have achieved a nice, crisp-cut form, use a small plane to bring it to shape and a scrap of fine-grade sandpaper to rub it down to a smooth, round-edged finish (see Fig. 5-7).

Special Tip

When making small component parts that will be drilled, as with the connecting rod, where the drilled holes are very near the edge, it's all the more important to choose your wood with great care. You need wood that is strong both along the run of the grain and across short-grained areas, such as plum, box, or sycamore.

5. Cut the plunger block out on the scroll saw, and use a large-size Forstner bit to lower the linkage step to a depth of slightly lower than ³/₁₆ inch. Test-fit the connecting rod in the plunger recess and see how everything comes together (see Fig. 5-8).

6. Drill the ¼-inch-diameter hole through the plunger block, and fit the dowel stub. Have the stub set lower

Fig. 5-7. *Use a fold of fine-grade sandpaper to rub the edges down to a rounded finish.*

Fig. 5-8. *Use a square or a metal straightedge to check the alignment.*

than the face of the block so that it finishes up slightly lower than the top face of the connecting rod. Test-fit to make sure the two parts come together for a smooth running action (see Fig. 5-9).

Turning the Drive Wheel

1. Take the blank that you have cut out on the scroll saw, and use a 2-inch-diameter Forstner bit to sink a hole in the best face to a depth of ¼ inch (see Fig. 5-10).

2. Change the jaws of the lathe chuck so that it can be used in the expansive mode. Locate the jaws in the drilled hole, and secure the blank with the back facing the bed of the lathe (see Fig. 5-11).

3. Turn the back of the blank to a smooth finish, and clean up the edges so that you have a disk 3¼ inches in diameter.

4. Remove the disk, change the jaws, and remount with the drilled face toward the bed of the lathe. Turn the drilled hole out so that it is 2¼ inches in diameter, and generally bring all the edges to a round-cornered finish (see Fig. 5-12).

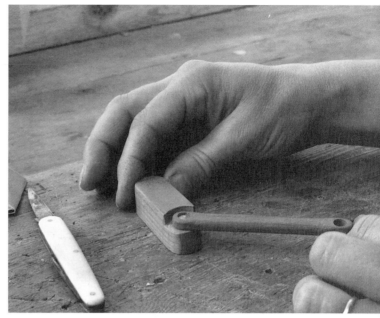

Fig. 5-9. Test for free movement at the pivot. The connecting rod should be able to almost angle around to 90 degrees to the plunger block.

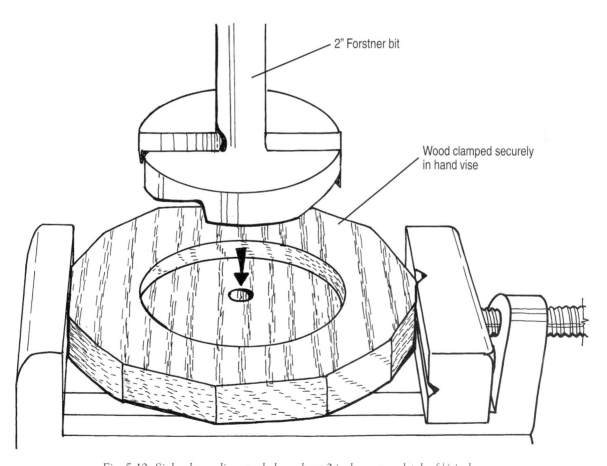

2" Forstner bit

Wood clamped securely in hand vise

Fig. 5-10. Sink a large-diameter hole—about 2 inches—to a depth of ¼ inch.

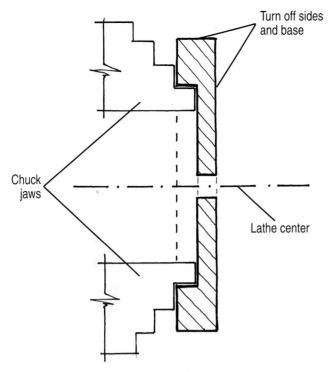

Turn off sides and base

Chuck jaws

Lathe center

Fig. 5-11. Set the chuck jaws in the hole, and wind them out so that the disk is held secure.

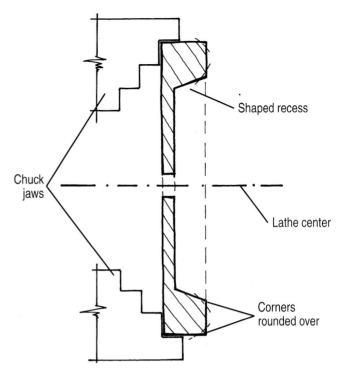

Shaped recess

Chuck jaws

Lathe center

Corners rounded over

Fig. 5-12. Grip the disk in the jaws of the chuck, and turn the drilled hole out to a dished section, as shown in the working drawing cross section.

5.   While the lathe is up and running, turn the little barrel shape that goes to make the knob.

6.   Test-fit to see how the three components come together. Adjust for a good fit (see Fig. 5-13).

Fitting, Assembly, and Finishing

1.   Set all the blocks in place in the box, and hold them secure with the dowels. Don't glue them at this stage.

Fig. 5-13. Check the various levels to make sure there is a smooth and easy movement.

2.   Cut the wheel pivot dowel to size, run a ⅛-inch-diameter hole through its top end for a little fixing peg, and glue it in place in the base slab. Set the wheel on the pivot and secure it with the fixing pin (see Fig. 5-14).

Special Tip

With small projects like this one, that need lots of small dowels and wooden pins, a good, inexpensive source is to use the sort of sticks that you can buy for cocktails, barbecues, and kabobs. They are often a bit oval in cross section and might need reshaping, but they are usually made from a hardwood like beech and serve the purpose well.

3.   Link the connecting rod to the wheel with the pivot and the knob, and fit with a little holding pin (see Fig. 5-15). Perform a trial turn to make sure that everything runs smoothly.

4.   Having fitted the plunger, the connecting rod, and the turning knob, remove the knob with its pivot, and then cut the clear sheet to shape and slide it in place (see Fig. 5-16). If any of the fixing dowels touch the plastic, lower them some.

5.   With the plastic sheet in place, refit the knob so as to link up the connecting rod and the wheel (see Fig. 5-17).

Fig. 5-14. Run the little pin through the dowel so that the wheel is held secure.

Fig. 5-15. Test the movement. If need be, adjust the sides of the blocks, the top of the plunger block, or both.

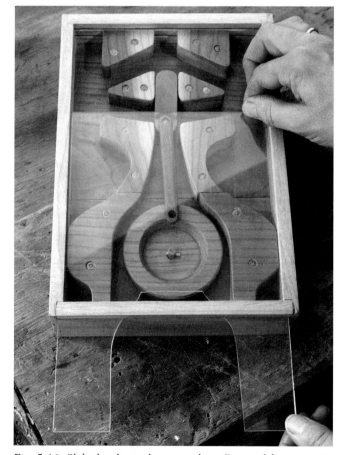

Fig. 5-16. Slide the plastic sheet into place. Be careful not to twist or force the now-delicate side pieces.

Fig. 5-17. Finally, glue the little pin in place.

6. If all is correct, glue everything in place, wax everything to a burnished finish, drop the marbles in place, and the plunger is ready for plunging.

Afterthoughts and Troubleshooting

• One problem with this project is that you have to do so many trial fittings to get everything up and running. This is why all the gluing should be left until the end.

• One of the best ways of cutting dowels to length is to use a fat-bladed knife and roll them on a flat surface. The cutting action of the thick-angled knife bevel results in the dowels being nicely domed at the ends.

• Cutting the shape in the plastic sheet was a real bear. After making a complete mess-up of one sheet, I fitted a special plastic-cutting blade in the scroll saw, and this time it went fine.

• When you are working with the plastic sheet, the biggest problem is avoiding scratching the surface. Don't be tempted to peel off the protective paper; it's best to leave it on until the very end.

Projects

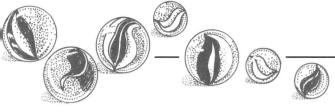

Marble Coordination Tester

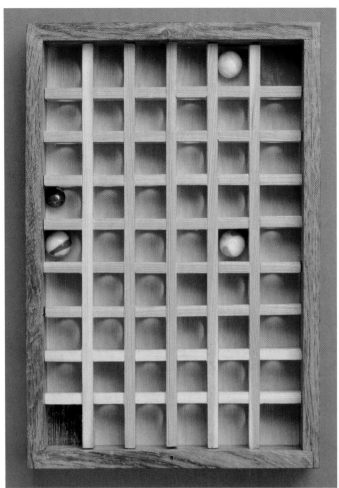

Marble Deceleration
Honeycomb Maze

Ultimate-Level
Marble Labyrinth

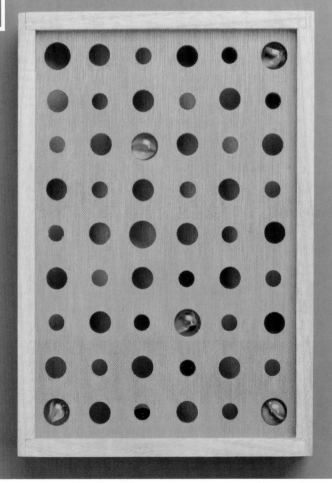

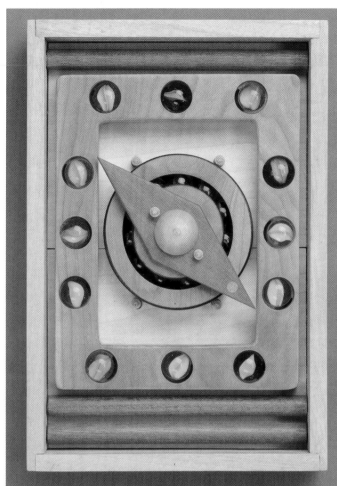

Marble-Bearing
Random Number Selector

Marble Ejector

Perpetual Marble Delivery Device

Marble Rotator Finger-Touch Tumbler Labyrinth

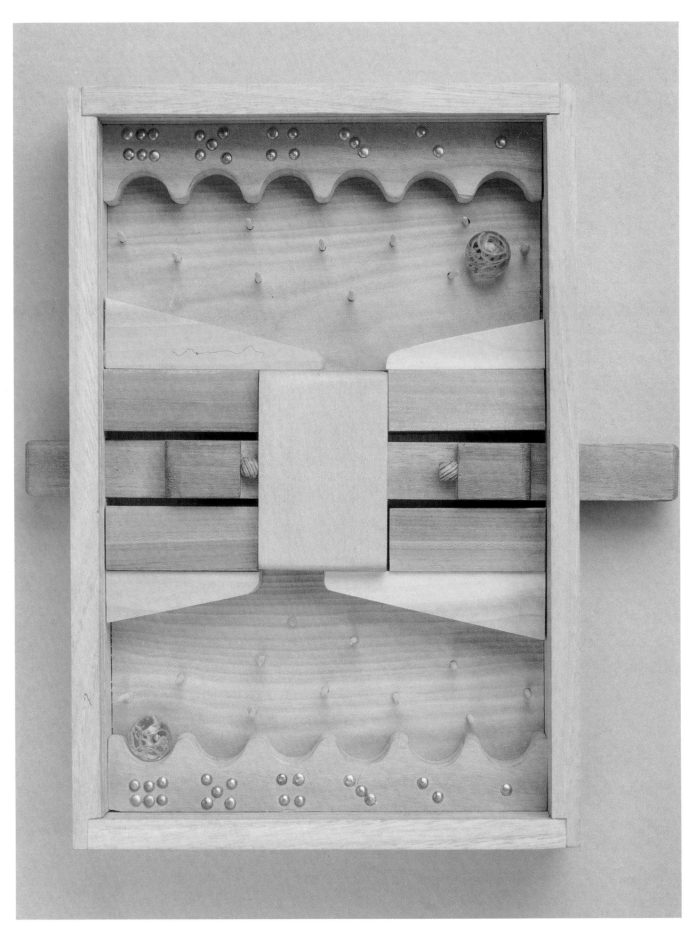

Perpetual Random Number Shuffler

A No-Nonsense, No-Purpose, Ball-Bearing Shifter Contraption

The Magnificent Goldberg-Robinson-Williamson
Marble-Kicking Device

Project 6
....

Perpetual Marble Delivery Device

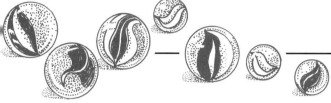

This device almost certainly draws its inspiration from the bubble gum machines we were all fascinated by when we were kids. All you did was put a penny in the slot and turn the handle, and presto, a brightly colored gum ball and maybe a little prize would roll down a chute and drop into your hot, sticky little hands. And woe betide the machine if it didn't cough up!

The Perpetual Marble Delivery Device is a beautifully complete machine, perfectly mirror imaged and reversed. In action, you stand the box upright on one end, turn the knob at the side until a marble is gobbled up, and continue turning until the machine shoots the marble out at the bottom. When all the marbles have been digested and delivered, you then turn the machine up the other way and start over. This is a great device for whiling away the hours. If you are looking for a bit of light relief between reading Tolstoy's *War and Peace* and Bertrand Russell's *Principia Mathematics*, then this is the project for you.

Design, Structure, and Techniques

The beauty of this project is the way that the marbles are channeled down the chute and passed one at a time through the selector box. If you look at the working drawings (see Fig. 6-1, 6-2, and 6-3), you will see that it's a beautiful little apparatus that has to do with the intersection and interplay of three perfectly drilled holes. All you have, in fact, is a main block with one hole drilled through horizontally for the selector spindle and another drilled through vertically for the chute, with the selector spindle or shaft being drilled with a marble-sized pocket hole that runs partway through its diameter. The diameter of the spindle shaft steps out and widens as it enters the selector block.

In action, the marble drops down the top feed chute and into the spindle pocket, the spindle turns until the pocket hole lines up with the bottom chute, and the marble drops down and out. As this is an ongoing action, there are always three marbles on the move: one in the top chute, another in the spindle pocket, and yet another being shot out at the bottom (see Fig. 6-3). The success of the project hinges on your being able to do the lathe work, and drill smooth-sided holes using Forstner bits.

The rest of the design is pretty straightforward, no more than a collection of blocks set in and around the spindle shaft to contain and direct the marbles. The four holes with their captive marbles are simply decorative, but the rows of spiked dowels are functional in that they act as a fence to prevent the marbles from rolling between the top of the blocks and the clear plastic sheet.

If you look at the working drawings, you will see that we have avoided covering them with measurements. The flexible design allows you to more or less change the measurements to suit your own needs. For example, you might use different size marbles, you might have a range of different size drill bits, and so on. Study our design, and then use it as a springboard for your own variations.

Choosing the Wood

You need to choose the wood for this project with great care. You need easy-to-turn wood for the spindle, easy-to-drill wood for the selector block, and contrasting woods for the various guide blocks. We used 1¼-inch-square-section English beech for the spindle, scraps of European lime for the selector block and control knobs,

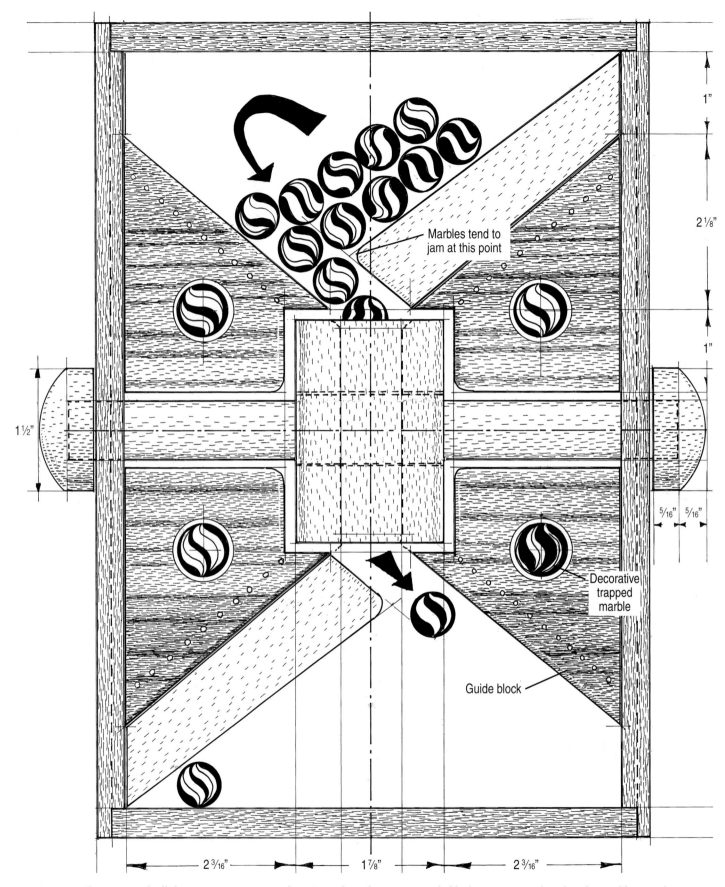

1"

2⅛"

1"

1½"

5/16" 5/16"

Marbles tend to
jam at this point

Decorative
trapped
marble

Guide block

2 3/16"   1 7/8"   2 3/16"

Fig. 6-1. Plan view with all the component parts in place. Note how the various guide blocks are arranged so that the marbles are always being fed into the chute.

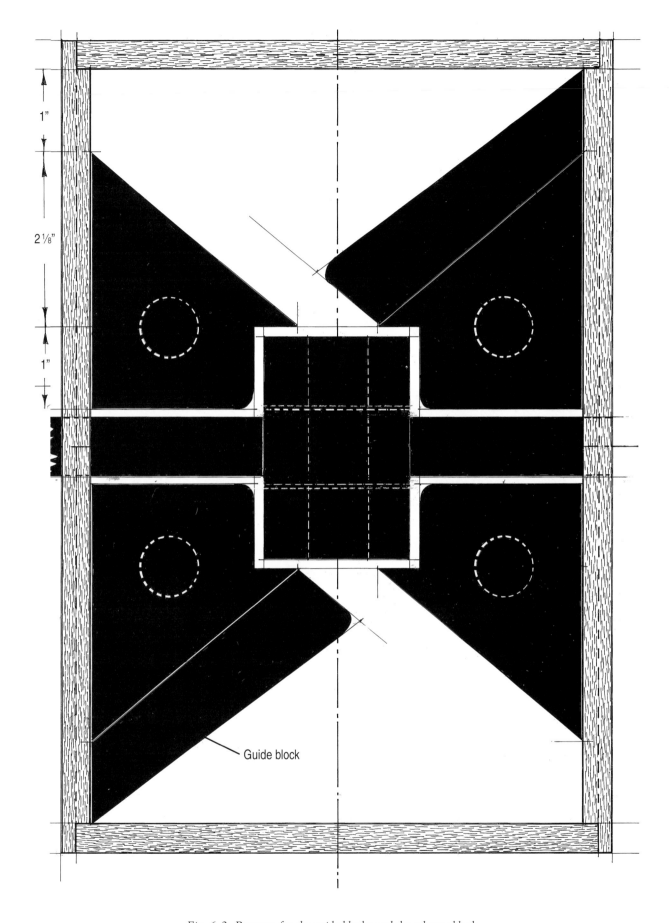

1"

2⅛"

1"

Guide block

Fig. 6-2. Patterns for the guide blocks and the selector block.

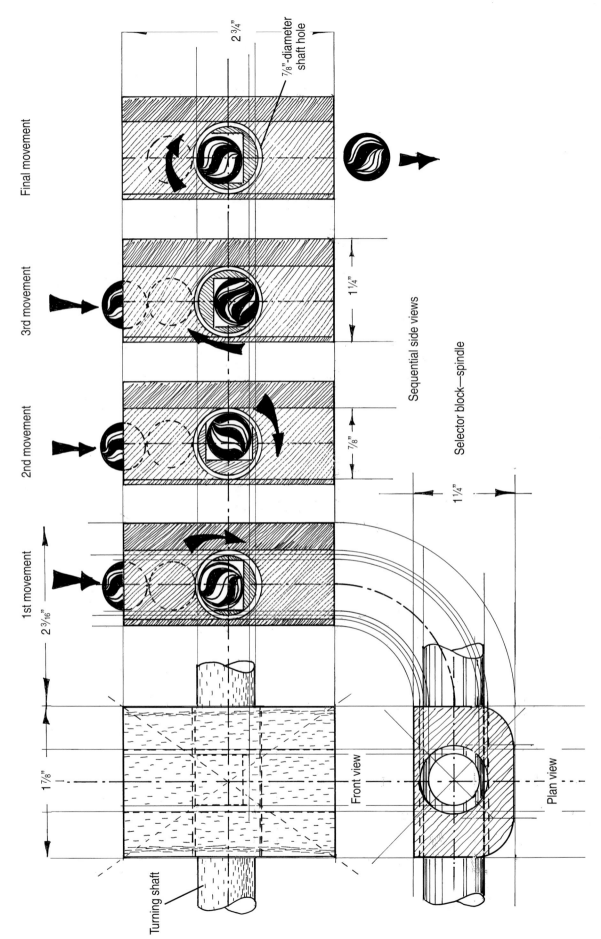

Final movement

3rd movement

2nd movement

1st movement

Sequential side views

Selector block—spindle

$2\frac{3}{4}$"

$\frac{7}{8}$"-diameter shaft hole

$1\frac{1}{4}$"

$\frac{7}{8}$"

$2\frac{3}{16}$"

$1\frac{7}{8}$"

$1\frac{1}{4}$"

Turning shaft

Front view

Plan view

Fig. 6-3. Front and plan views of the selector block, plus (left to right) the working sequence of the marble selector.

a ⅞-inch-thick slab of American tulip for the two pale-colored guide blocks, and ⅞-inch-thick American cherry for the four triangular guide blocks.

Making the Project
Turning the Spindle Shaft
1. Carefully study the working drawings (see Figs. 6-1, 6-2, and 6-3). Consider how the diameter of the shaft might well need to be modified to suit your range of drill bits. The easiest way of working is to measure the size of your chosen marbles, look at your selection of drill bits, and then size the shaft accordingly. Although we give diameters for the various holes—the vertical and horizontal holes through the block, the marble pocket holes, the holes through the side of the box, and all the rest—this is not to say that you can't change some hole sizes to suit. For example, we have used the same large size hole for the shaft to pass through the sides of the box and to fit the mushroom knobs, but there is no reason why you can't step the shaft down in diameter.

2. Take the length of square-section wood that you have chosen for the shaft, and mount it on the lathe between centers. Turn it down to a smooth cylinder, and size it to a diameter to suit the drill size you plan to use for drilling the horizontal block hole. We have gone for 1 inch.

3. Use the rule and dividers to mark the cylinder with all the step-offs that go to make up the design. Working from one end to the other, allow about 3 inches for one side, 1⅞ inches at the center, and 3 inches at the other side. This allows for knob spigots at both ends.

4. With the step-offs in place, turn the cylinder at each side of center down to ¾ inch in diameter (see Fig. 6-4) so that there is a spigot or step-up of ⅛ inch.

5. Use a pair of calipers to check the diameters, bring to a good finish, and then part off.

Turning the Mushroom Control Knobs
1. Mount the 1¾-inch-square section of wood on the lathe. It's best to put it in a four-jaw chuck at the headstock end.

2. Turn the wood down to a cylinder diameter of 1½ inches.

3. Working from the tailstock end, use a ruler and dividers to set out the seven ½-inch step-offs that go to make up the mushroom design. You need ½ inch for tailstock waste, two ½-inch step-offs for the first knob, ½ inch for between-knob waste, two more ½-inch step-offs for the other knob, and the rest for chuck waste.

4. Use a parting tool to lower the waste, then take the skew chisel and turn off the domed mushroom heads

Fig. 6-4. Use calipers to test the diameter of the turning. You should be aiming for a tight slip-fit within the points of the calipers.

of the two knobs. If you have the knobs set mirror-imaged facing each other (see Fig. 6-5), you will find that it's much easier to achieve a matching pair.

5. When you are happy with the profiles, bring the knob nearest the tailstock to a good finish, reduce the tailstock waste to nil, and carefully part off.

6. Finally, with the other half mushroom turning still supported in the chuck, wind the tailstock back out of the way, bring the other dome end to a good finish, and part off (see Fig. 6-6).

Making the Guide and the Selector Blocks
1. Check over the wood that you have chosen for the various blocks—the four triangular guide blocks, two wedge-shaped blocks, and two selector blocks. The idea of making two selector blocks is so that you can use one for trial drilling, just in case it doesn't work out.

2. Starting with the four large, triangular blocks, use a rule and pencil to lay out the measurements that go to make up the design. Label the blocks so that you know where they go in the scheme of things.

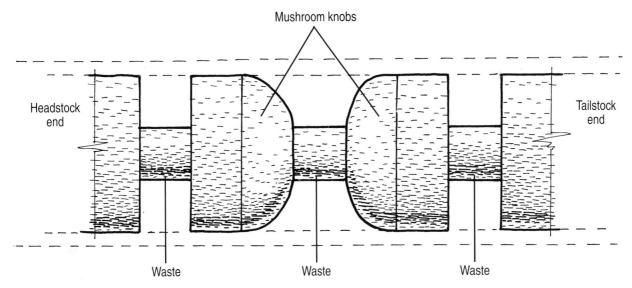

Mushroom knobs

Headstock
end

Tailstock
end

Waste

Waste

Waste

Fig. 6-5. *The easiest way to achieve a well-matched pair of knobs is to have them arranged in mirror-image fashion and then turn them both little by little.*

Fig. 6-6. *Turn the second knob to shape, and then part off.*

Fig. 6-7. *Sink the holes partway through the blocks. Set the depth stop so that they are all at the same depth.*

3. Cut out the basic forms on the scroll saw, and sink the blind holes for the captive marbles (see Fig. 6-7). Cut the other blocks out the same way.

4. Mount a sheet of fine-grade sandpaper with the grit side up on a piece of plywood, and use it to bring all the blocks to a good fit and finish (see Fig. 6-8). Mark out the position of the rows of wooden pins.

5. Drill two holes through the trial selector block: a 1-inch-diameter hole from side to side for the shaft and a ¾-inch-diameter hole from top to bottom for the

Fig. 6-8. *Rub down all the faces, edges, and sides on the sanding table. Aim for nicely rounded edges.*

Fig. 6-9. *When you are happy with the prototype selector block, then transfer all the measurements onto the good block and make it for real.*

marble chute. Also run shaft-size holes through the two long box sides.

6. Test-fit the various parts and see how they all come together. Pay particular attention to the fit of the shaft in the selector block.

7. When you are satisfied that all is correct and the various holes are neither too tight nor too loose, then transfer the measurements onto the good selector block and drill the holes (see Fig. 6-9).

Assembly and Finishing

1. When just about everything has been made, except for the marble pocket in the center of the shaft, and you have drilled and fitted the rows of wooden pins that run fencelike across the triangular blocks, then test-fit all the component parts.

2. With all the components in place, fit the two mushroom knobs so as to align the shaft in the selector block, and then establish the precise position of the marble pocket hole. This has to be done right the first time around, so spend time making sure that everything is just so (see Fig. 6-10).

3. Run the hole partway through the middle of the shaft so that the resultant pocket is big enough to take a marble. If all is correct, you should be able to drop a marble in the pocket within the shaft and then turn the shaft around in the block without the marble dragging or jamming up the works.

Fig. 6-10. *Fit all the component parts in the box. Make sure that the marbles flow down the chute, and establish the position of the marble pocket on the shaft.*

4. When you have achieved a good working fit, glue up the various component parts within the box, drill and fix the mushroom knobs on the ends of the spindle (see Fig. 6-11), and wax all the surfaces. Slide the clear plastic sheet in place, and your marble delivery device is up and running.

Fig. 6-11. Fit all the parts in place in the box. Glue the knobs on the ends of the shaft, and hold them in place with drilled and glued wooden pins.

Afterthoughts and Troubleshooting

• Though in many ways this design is pretty simple, the success of the project hinges on its being brought to a high degree of finish. As the entire works are on display, you have to take care that the forms are well made and give careful attention to detail.

• If ever you have doubts about tooling, design, or function, it's best to test everything out by making a prototype before making the real thing.

• If you decide to cut costs by buying your wood rough sawn, bear in mind that there will be a lot of waste: bark, split ends, knotty areas, and the like. Take this into account when you are comparing prices.

• A waxed finish is preferable for this project for the simple reason that varnish is liable to gum up the works, as it dribbles and has a thickness. Beeswax, on the other hand, is easy to apply and also helps ensure that the moving parts function smoothly.

• The marbles may get lodged in the chutes, so when you are playing, joggle the box to keep the marbles on the move.

Project 7

Marble Rotator Finger-Touch Tumbler Labyrinth

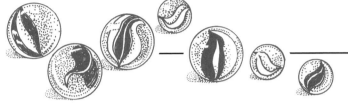

This project draws its inspiration from the cops-and-robbers films I used to watch when I was a kid—the kind where a group of bad guys plan to break into a bank vault. At the climax of the film, the safecracker—usually a sweaty guy with a gun, a drinking problem, and an evil temper—puts his ear to the safe, turns the dial, and listens to the tumblers as they drop. After several close-up shots of various members of the group showing lots of fumbling fingers, wild eyes, and beard stubble, the door of the safe swings open, and guess what? The alarm bell goes off! Anyway, it got me wondering about the tumblers—is it as easy as it looks?

The exciting thing about this labyrinth project, the thing that gives it that extra twist, is that you can't see what's going on. You can hear the marble clunk as you turn the dial this way and that, and to some extent you can feel the vibrations as the marble rolls along, but you can't see anything except the control cord running around the various wheels as you turn the dial. The object of the game—the challenge and the adventure—is to get the marble in the side hole and then route it through the maze until you can see it in the spy hole, and then back again.

So if you've always fantasized about safecracking your way into a comfortable retirement, then this project is for you.

Design, Structure, and Techniques

This project is pretty difficult to make. Not only does it involve turning and fretting, but getting the cord around the various wheels is truly finger-twistingly tricky. The problem is that by the time you have set the wheels in place on their pivots, tied on the cord, and eased the pivots out so that you can slide the cage in place, the whole thing is threatening to come apart. The cord gets tangled up, falls off the wheel, and becomes knotted. It's a difficult challenge. It's helpful to use waxed cord and a length of bent wire for a needle. The good thing about the waxed cord is that you can stroke it into shape so that an inch or two is self-supporting.

As for the wood-turning procedures, one look at the photographs will show you that turning the thin walls that go to make the maze is no easy matter. Not only do you need to use a four-jaw chuck and have a steady hand, but more than that, the wood needs to be perfect, with no splits or knots.

Choosing the Wood

Apart from the box itself, we chose to use five different woods in all. We used best-quality 1-inch-thick European beech for the tumbler maze wheel, 1¾-inch-square-section American cherry for the four pulley wheels, ¼-inch-thick larch for the base slab, ⅛-inch multicore plywood for the cage front, and ¼-inch multicore plywood for the large dial wheel.

Multicore plywood means European or American plywood that is made up from lots of thin veneer layers of birch wood. For example, the ¼-inch ply has five layers. It's important that you don't use soft-core plywood such as that from Malaysia. Certainly such ply is a fraction of the cost of multicore, but it is full of insect holes, it is so soft and fluffy that it is almost impossible to bring to a good finish, and most annoying of all, it is liable to snap. Multicore, on the other hand, is incredibly strong in all directions, it leaves the scroll saw with the sawn edge being so smooth that is only needs a minimum of finishing, the pale color is attractive, and it is generally pleasant to work.

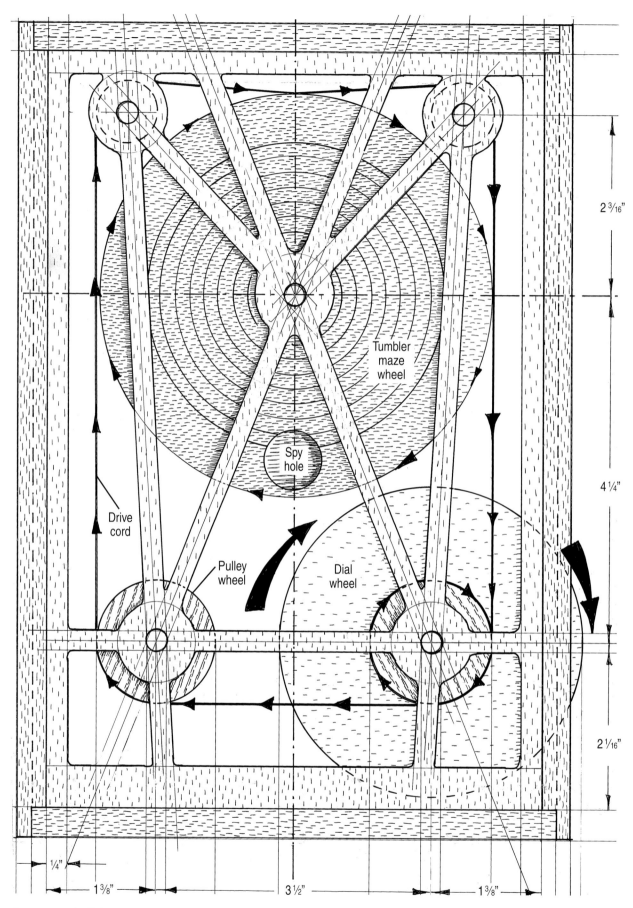

Fig. 7-1. Plan view with all the component parts in place. Note the route the cord takes as it travels around the various wheels—how it travels right around the maze wheel and the dial wheel.

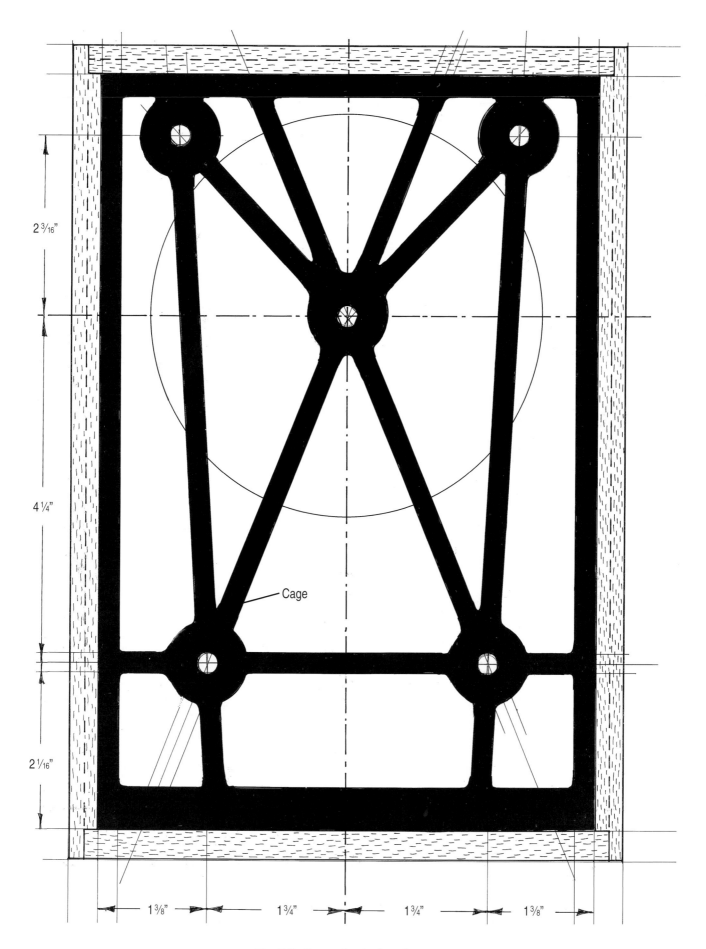

Fig. 7-2. Pattern for the fretted cage.

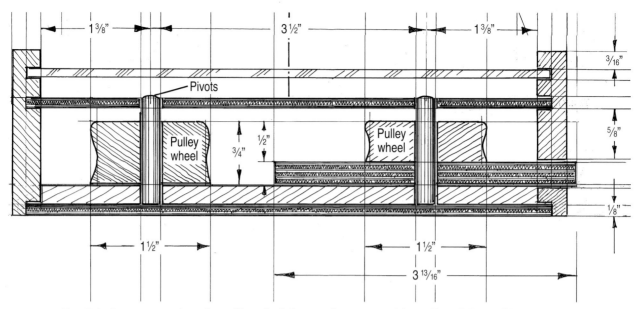

Fig. 7-3. Cross section through tumbler wheel showing the position of the walls and the marble escape route.

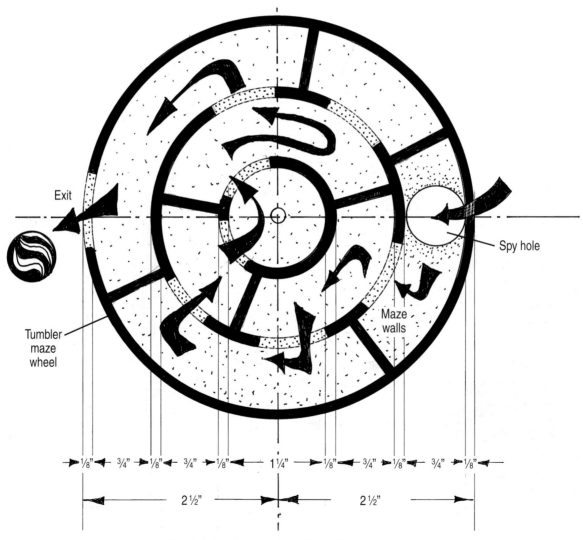

Fig. 7-4. Section view through tumbler maze.

Making the Project
Turning the Maze Wheel

1. Having made the basic box and planed the baseboard to a good fit, use a compass, rule, and pencil to mark in the position of the pivot points for the disk and the four pulleys, and run them through with a ¼-inch-diameter drill bit.

2. Take a good, long look at the working drawings (see Figs. 7-1, 7-2, 7-3, and 7-4), and see how the disk needs to be worked. Note how it is held in a four-jaw chuck to avoid having fixing holes.

3. When you are clear as to how to proceed, take the piece of 1-inch-thick wood that you have chosen for the maze wheel, draw out the disks, and cut it to size on the scroll saw. It needs to be 5¾ inches in diameter.

4. Mount the disk on the lathe, and turn it down to a smooth disk of 5 inches in diameter and ⅞ inch thick. Bring the best face to a good, smooth finish, and then lay out rings spaced at ¼-inch intervals. Make sure that the center point is clearly established (see Fig. 7-5).

5. When you are happy with the front face, cut a V-section groove around the edge for the cord track, then turn the disk over in the chuck and bring the back face to a smooth finish.

6. Lay out the channels with the rule and dividers: the walls at ⅛ inch thick, two channels at ¾ inch wide, and the center at 1¼ inches diameter. Then use the parting tool to sink the waste.

7. Repeatedly check the depth and width of the channels to ensure that there will be plenty of room for the marble to move (see Fig. 7-6).

8. Finally, sand the disk to a good finish and remove from the lathe.

Building the Maze

1. Study the working drawing (see Fig. 7-4), noting how the basic turning needs to be modified, with walls cut away and barriers added. Then mark in the position of the spy hole, the exit arch, where the walls need to be cut away for passages, and so on. It's best to position

Fig. 7-5. Turn the face to a good, smooth finish, and then cut the decorative lines at ¼-inch intervals. Make sure that the center point is clearly marked.

Fig. 7-6. Use a parting tool to sink the marble channels. Aim for a depth of about ⅝ inch so that there is a wood thickness to the face of the disk of about 3/16 inch.

Fig. 7-7. Use a forstner bit to sink the ¾-inch-diameter spy hole. Have a piece of waste wood inside the channel, and work slowly to avoid splitting the wood.

Fig. 7-8. Use a razor-sharp chisel to pare out the gaps in the walls. Don't try to slice the waste out in one great thrust, but rather, break the top of the wall with a line of cuts, then skim out and make more cuts, and so on, so that the waste is removed in fine layers.

Fig. 7-9. Mark in the position of the barrier walls, and then fill them in with little ¾-inch-wide strips.

the spy hole in line with the run of the grain, either vertically or horizontally.

2. To drill the spy hole, set a waste block in the channel, and drill a ¾-inch-diameter hole through from the front face (see Fig. 7-7). Go at it every slowly so as not to split the wood or run off course.

3. Use a coping saw to cut the exit arch through the wall, on the other side of the disk opposite the drilled hole. For example, if the drilled hole is at 6 o'clock, then the arch needs to be at 12 o'clock.

4. Use a sharp chisel to carefully pare away selected chunks of wall (see Fig. 7-8), creating a marble-width passage.

5. Mark in the position of the barrier walls (see Fig. 7-9), then cut little ¾-inch-long strips of wood to fit, and glue them in place across the marble channels. This procedure is tricky and sticky, so take your time cutting all the pieces to fit before you start spreading the glue.

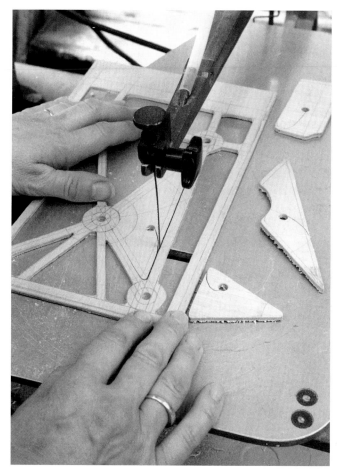

Fig. 7-10. Hold the workpiece firmly and flat down on the saw table, and fret out the windows of waste. Be careful that the saw blade doesn't jolt the workpiece out of your hands and break the slender sections.

> **Special Tip**
>
> There are glues, glues, and more glues, some of them good, some bad, and some terrible. For projects of this kind, we recommend instant superglue for small tacking tasks and white polyvinyl acetate (PVA) glue for the rest.

Fretting the Cage

1.   Study the working drawing (see Fig. 7-2), then take the drilled baseboard and use it to transfer the position of the drilled pivot holes onto the sheet of ⅛-inch-thick plywood. This done, use a pencil, measure, and rule to lay out all the lines that go to make up the design of the cage.

2.   Run the five pivot holes through with the ¼-inch-diameter drill bit, and then run pilot holes through each of the "windows" of waste that need to be cut away.

3.   Use a pencil, rule, and compass to draw in all the lines of the design.

4.   Cut out each of the waste windows as follows. Slacken off the blade tension, and unhitch the bottom end of the blade. Pass the blade through the pilot hole, refit the blade, and retension. Run the line of cut to the waste side of the drawn line (see Fig. 7-10).

5.   Once you have fretted out the eleven windows of waste, sand the sawn edges to a smooth finish, and test-fit the pieces (see Fig. 7-11).

Making the Control Wheels

1.   Look at the working drawings, and note how there are five control wheels in all. There are four turned pulley wheels—two small ones ¾ inches in diameter at the top and two large ones 1½ inches in diameter at the bottom—and a large plywood dial wheel 3³⁄₁₆ inches in diameter.

2.   Start by cutting out the dial wheel. Simply draw it out with the compass, fret the resultant disk out on the scroll saw, and then sand it to a good, smooth finish. It can be made quicker than the telling.

3.   Take another look at the working drawing (see Fig. 7-1), and note the dimension of the four pulley wheels. See that although three of the four wheels are ¾ inch thick, so that they will fit nicely between the base slab and the plywood cage, the wheel that is to be mounted on top of the ¼-inch-thick plywood disk is only ½ inch thick.

4.   Mount the 1¾-inch-square-section wood between lathe centers, and turn it down to a smooth cylinder 1½ inches in diameter.

Fig. 7-11. Check the position of the various components, and cut the dowel pivots to length.

Fig. 7-12. Use a parting chisel to skim the ends of the pulley wheels to a clean finish so that they fit nicely between the baseboard and the cage plywood.

5. Use the rule and dividers to lay out the cylinder with all the step-offs that go to make up the design. Working from the tailstock end, allow ¼ inch for tailstock waste, ¾ inch for the first small pulley, ¼ inch for parting waste, ¾ inch for the next small pulley, ¼ inch for parting waste, ¾ inch for the first large pulley, ¼ inch for parting waste, ¾ inch for the other large pulley, and the rest for headstock waste.

6. Use a parting tool to sink the waste to a depth of ½ inch, so that you are left with a central core ½ inch in diameter.

7. Turn the four pulley blanks down to profile so that they are rounded at the corners and slightly dipped at the center (see Fig. 7-12).

8. Part the pulleys off one at a time, being sure to mark the center points. And when you get to the pulley nearest the headstock, skim a ¼-inch slice off its thickness.

9. Glue the modified pulley wheel to the best face of the plywood dial wheel, so that the skimmed face of the pulley is facing the ply, and drill out all the pivot holes at ¼ inch diameter.

Assembly and Stringing Up

1. All the component parts that go to make up the project should be nicely finished and waxed. Be careful that you don't get wax on the edge of the maze wheel—meaning in the V track—or on the edge of the dial wheel. Then set the baseboard in the box, pop the five pivot dowels in position, and set the maze wheel and the other wheels in place.

2. Take a look at the working drawing (see Fig. 7-1), and see how the little arrows on the cord mark out its route. If you start at the pulley at bottom left, the cord goes up to the pulley at top left, right around the maze wheel, on around the pulley at top right, down and around the dial wheel pulley, and back to the pulley at bottom left. When you have routed the cord as shown, tie it off with a slipknot and leave it with long ends (see Fig. 7-13).

3. Gently ease the pivots out, so that the wheels more or less stay in place, and then slide the fretted plywood cage in place.

4. Now for the tricky part. One at a time, dab the ends of the pivots in PVA glue, and slide them home through the cage holes, on through the wheels, and on

Fig. 7-13. Use a barbecue stick to ease the cords into place. Note the slipknot and the long cord ends.

into the baseboard. This isn't easy! You will find that it's relatively easy to get four of the pivots in place, but the fifth one will be tricky. The cord will come off, the pivots will jump out of their holes, and so on.

5. Once everything is in place, make sure that the cord is on track, then ease the cord ends around so that they are within reach. Tighten up the slipknot, tie off, and trim back (see Fig. 7-14).

6. Slide the clear plastic sheet into place, and the game is ready for playing.

Afterthoughts and Troubleshooting

• The working action of this project requires that the cord be smooth-running and frictionless over the two small pulley wheels and the large pulley at bottom left, while at the same time, there needs to be a good amount of friction around the maze wheel and the dial wheel. To achieve this, you need to wax the pulley wheels and leave the maze wheel and the dial wheel unwaxed. The cord must be fine, strong, and fray-proof. We experimented with various kinds and found that the best is the stiff, waxed linen cord used by shoemakers.

• One problem is that the pivots want to lift up out of their holes. To prevent this, wedge them in place in the cage holes. To make a wedge, sharpen a sliver of wood to a point, dip the point in glue, push and wedge the glued tip in the cage pivot hole alongside the pivot, and trim off.

Fig. 7-14. Use two sticks to lift up the cord ends, and then tighten up the slipknot and knot off.

Perpetual Random Number Shuffler

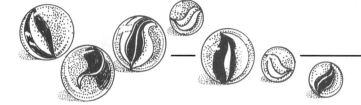

There I was last Christmas—full of food, half asleep, and nicely comfortable in my chair—when the family insisted that I pull myself together and join in a game of Monopoly. Okay, so I enjoy a good board game as much as the next guy, but the hard work and tedium of throwing the dice is sometimes just too much. And then it came to me: Here we were on the brink of the twenty-first century, still throwing numbered "knuckle bones," much as our ancestors must have done way back in the dark ages, when it all could be done mechanically.

As I chewed on another piece of mince pie, I pondered long and hard, my mind running at full power. A steam-driven dice thrower maybe, with pistons delivering the dice. Or I could harness the power of the wind. Or design a water-driven turbine. Or perhaps I could build something really big, with lots of strings, mirrors, and levers, or even a computer-driven arrangement. After a lot of thought and another glass of cider, I came up with the Perpetual Random Number Shuffler.

In action, you hold it on end, push the shuffler rod in to deliver the first marble, pull the rod back to load the other marble into the chamber, and then push the rod to deliver the second marble. When the marbles drop down, they bounce off the pattern of wooden pins and fall at random into the scooped number pockets. When you are ready for the next throw, you simply flip the box over and start again. The skill is in being able to jolt the box this way and that to send the marbles into the pockets of your choice.

It has been pointed out to me by my disparaging family that throwing a pair of dice is altogether less strain on the brain and wrist than building a box, heav-ing the box around, and then pushing and pulling rods and all. But it's not half the fun.

Design, Structure, and Technique

To my mind, the great thing about this project is the satisfying way the shuffler rod works with a pull-push action to drop the marbles—one pull to load the chamber and one push to eject the marble. It feels good, the way the movement of the rod is governed by having stops that clunk up against the box and chamber. And then again, the marbles make a very satisfying *ping* when they bounce in and around the pattern of wooden pins. All in all, it's a very "touch, hear, and enjoy" machine.

The design is slightly unusual in that the baseboard is made in two parts and dropped in at either side of the chamber, so as to bring the surface holding the wooden pins closer to the face of the box, and also to give a good thickness of wood to hold the pins (see Fig. 8-4).

The chamber itself is surprisingly easy to make. All it is, in effect, is a block with a chiseled channel, with two holes running into the channel—one at the left and one at the right of the centerline. The only tricky part of the construction is putting the stops on the through-rod so that the through-rod hole is perfectly aligned with the chamber holes. If you look at the drawings, you can see that the working action is beautifully direct. The marble drops down the hole at one side of the chamber, the rod captures the marble, and the moving rod drags the marble across and drops it down the other hole. Though this sounds simple enough, the trick is being able to adjust the stops so that the rod is in the right place at the right time.

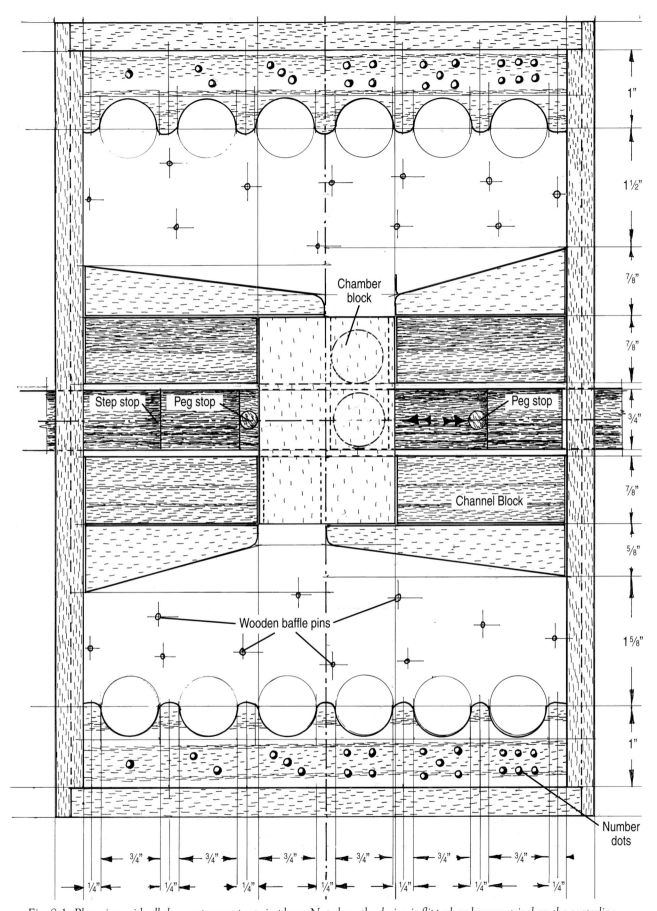

Fig. 8-1. Plan view with all the component parts in place. Note how the design is flipped and symmetrical on the centerline.

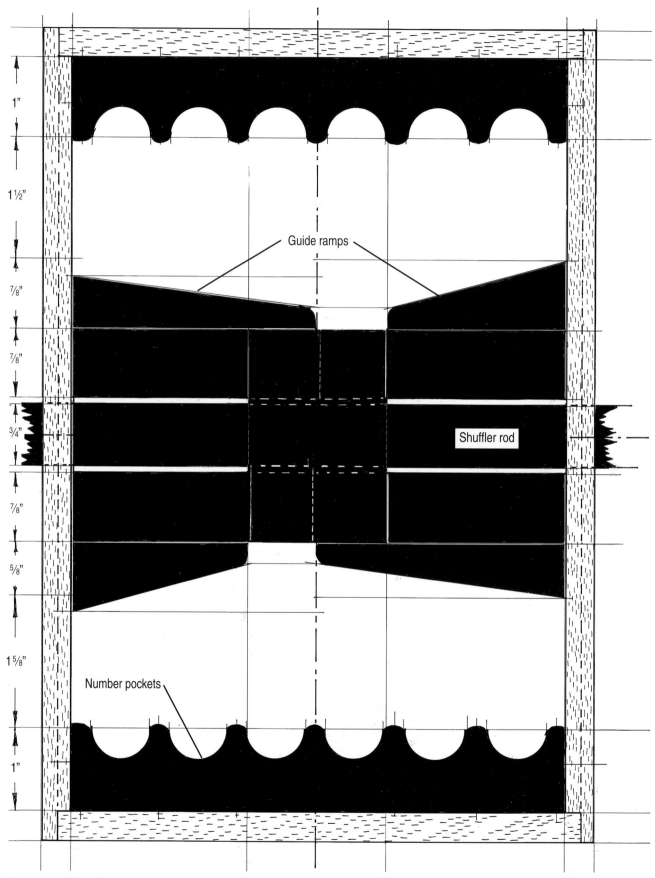

Fig. 8-2. Patterns for the main components. The chamber block, the shuffler rod, the four channel blocks, the four sloping guide ramps, and the two pocket strips.

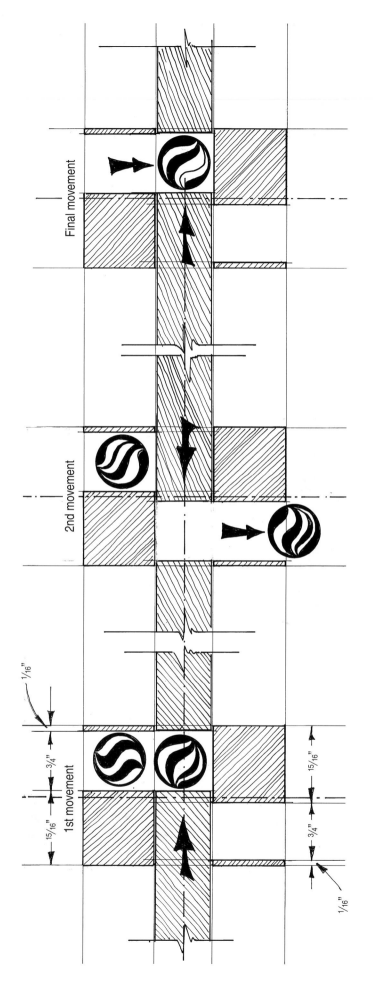

Fig. 8-3. Cross-section view showing the working action of the shuffler rod within the chamber.

The tooling is straightforward enough. You need to use a scroll saw and a drill press with Forstner bits, and you also need to know how to pare with a chisel.

If you have any doubts about getting the working action right, or you aren't quite sure what goes where and how, the best thing to do is to build a prototype from pieces of waste wood. Once you've figured out the workings of the chamber and the positions of the holes and the stops, the rest is easy.

Note: Don't put the actual box together until the bridge holes are cut in the side pieces.

Choosing the Wood

The design of this project is such that you can use a good number of pieces of contrasting wood to achieve a dynamic effect. We used ¾-inch-thick tulip wood for the four sloping guide blocks, ⅞-inch-thick American cherry heartwood for the four channel blocks, 1¼-inch-thick oak for the shuffler-rod, 1¼-inch-thick lime for the chamber block, ¾-inch-thick pale American cherry for the two scooped pocket pieces, and a thin pine board for the two baseboards.

The secret of success here is in choosing nicely colored wood that is as nearly as possible free from knots. Above all, the wood must cut clean. There are enough problems without your having to worry about the wood splitting or being too difficult to cut.

Making the Project
Making the Chamber Block

Take a good, long look at the working drawings (see Figs. 8-1, 8-2, and 8-3) and the illustration showing the arrangement of the component parts within the box (see Fig. 8-4). When you have gathered all your carefully selected pieces of wood, take a piece of 1¼-inch-thick wood that you have chosen for the chamber block, cut it to size, and bring it to a good, true, and smooth finish.

2. Round over the top and bottom face edges as shown, and lay it out with crossed centerlines to mark the vertical and horizontal axes. Draw in the position of the shuffler-rod channel, and mark the center points for the marble holes (see Fig. 8-5).

3. Take the marked-out block, run two saw lines at either side of the channel waste, on the waste side of the

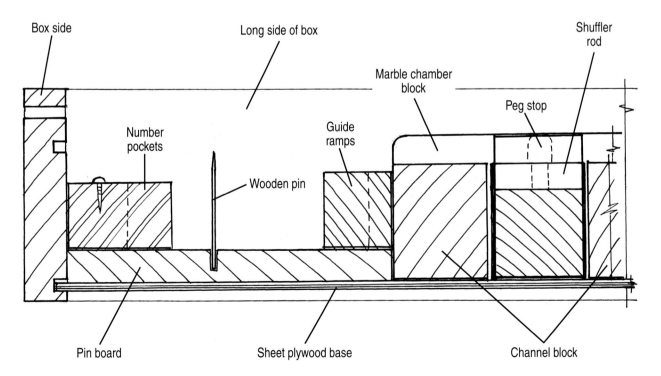

Fig. 8-4. The arrangement of the component parts.

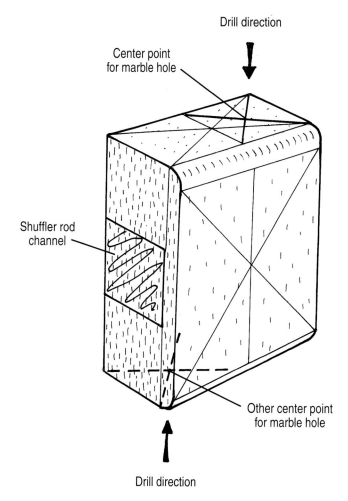

Drill direction

Center point
for marble hole

Shuffler rod
channel

Other center point
for marble hole

Drill direction

Fig. 8-5. The centerlines and the layout lines for the chamber
block.

Fig. 8-6. Pare the channel out with a bevel-edged chisel. Skim the
base of the channel to a smooth finish, first from one end and
then from the other.

drawn lines, and then clear the channel with a ¾-inch-
wide bevel-edged chisel (see Fig. 8-6). The fit must be
good, so work slowly. If you have doubts about your paring skills, work well to the waste sides of the drawn lines
and sand back to a good fit.

4. Now move to the drill press, and run ¾-inch-
diameter holes down through into the end grain and on
into the channel (see Fig. 8-7). The good news is that
though drilling into end grain is sometimes hard going,
you don't have to worry about the bit splitting the grain
as it exits. The bit will always exit cleanly.

5. Sand all the faces to a good finish.

Making and Fitting the Shuffler Rod

1. Start by planing the wood to a clean, 1¼-by-1-
inch cross section, with all the faces being true. This
done, cautiously plane back the sides so that the thickness is reduced to fit the chamber channel, finishing up
close to ¾ inch wide. The working action relies on the
fit being good, so spend time getting it right.

Fig. 8-7. Align the drill bit on the center point, and run the hole
through to the channel.

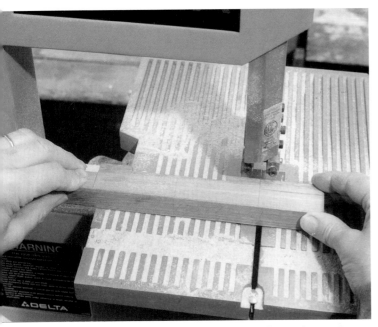

Fig. 8-8. *Whereas the central area needs to be cut first on the band saw and then pared down with the chisel, the end waste can be cleared with two cuts on the band saw.*

2. Set the 1¼-by-¾-inch section side-down on the bench, and use a square and rule to set out the position of the stepped blocks. The trick is positioning the stepped stop just so, but the little pegs do allow for a good margin of error. Though the outside face of the step must be well placed so that the rod clunks against the inside face of the box when the holes are all nicely aligned, the peg stops can be positioned slightly this way or that to suit (see Figs. 8-1, 8-2, and 8-3).

3. When you are happy with the lines of the design, cut them in on the band saw (see Fig. 8-8), and then pare back the waste with the chisel and shoulder plane. Make sure that the wood on either side of the stepped stops is a nice ¾-by-¾-inch-square section so that it will fit the chamber channel and the holes that will be cut in the sides of the box.

4. Halve the distance between the stops, and run a ¾-inch-diameter hole through the width of the rod. Make fine adjustments by fitting two peg stops so that they clunk against the sides of the chamber block to bring the rod and chamber holes into alignment (see Fig. 8-9).

5. Set the chamber block in place on the base of the box, meaning the thin sheet of plywood, and fine-tune the position of the peg and step stops (see Fig. 8-10). If you need to ease the setting because the holes are slightly out of true, pare the stepped steps back and/or skim one side of the pegs down to a flat face.

6. Take the two long sides of the box, and cut a 1-by-¾-inch bridge hole at the center bottom. Pare the hole to a crisp finish (see Fig. 8-11). Note that the inch measurement allows the shuffler rod to fit flush when the plywood sheet is in place.

Cutting the Scooped Marble Pockets

1. If you have a look at the working drawings (see Figs. 8-1, 8-2, and 8-3), you will see that the scooped pockets are based on a row of ¾-inch-diameter circles set ¼ inch apart.

2. Take your ¾-inch-thick wood, and cut and plane it to a width of 1 inch. Draw a line about ³⁄₁₆ inch back from one edge, and mark step-offs of ¼ inch, ⅜ inch, ⅜ inch, ¼ inch, ⅜ inch, ⅜ inch, ¼ inch, and so on along the lines. Then use a compass or dividers to draw the circles.

3. Fret the two six-circle strips out on the scroll saw, and rub them to a good finish.

4. Drill the pattern of number holes on each strip, one running from 1 to 6 and the other from 6 to 1, and then push the brass-headed nails home.

Assembly and Finishing

1. Take another look at the working drawings (see Figs. 8-1, 8-2, 8-3, and 8-4), and note how the various components all relate to one another. For example, the shuffler rod, the chamber block, and the four channel

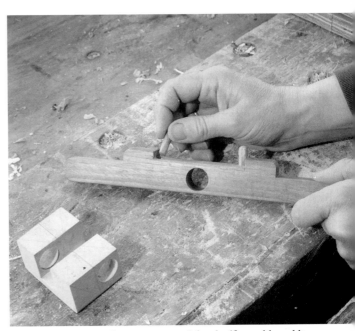

Fig. 8-9. *Fine-tune the movement of the shuffler rod by adding small stop pegs.*

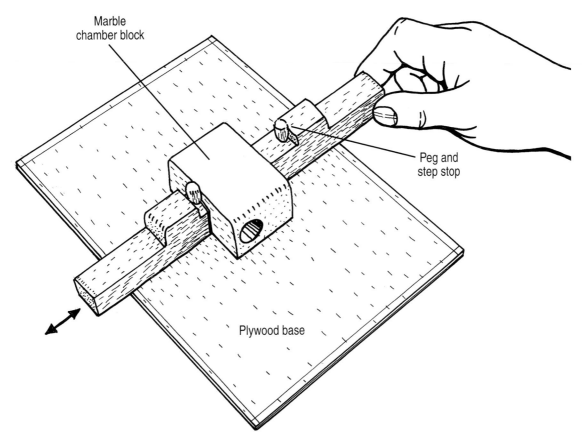

Marble
chamber block

Peg and
step stop

Plywood base

Fig. 8-10. Set the two components down on the plywood base, and test out the movement.

blocks are sitting directly on the plywood, and the pin boards fill the ends of the box, with the pocket strips and the sloped guides being set on top of the pin board. The middle-of-the-box edge of the pin boards acts as a stop to keep the channel blocks and the chamber block in position.

2. Take the ⅛-inch-thick boards, all nicely cut and planed to size, and drill the pattern of pin holes.

3. When you are ready to put everything together, set the shuffler rod across the box and in the bridge holes, and fit and nail the plywood baseboard in position.

4. Glue the drilled pin boards in place in the box.

5. Glue the chamber block and the channel blocks in place so that they are butted hard up against the edge of the pin boards, and then glue the pocket strips and the sloped guides in position on top of the boards. When you are satisfied with the arrangement, glue the pins in the pattern of holes (see Fig. 8-12).

6. Test the movement of the shuffler rod (see Fig. 8-13), making sure that the marbles can move freely through the pattern of pins and on down into the chamber. Then wax and burnish the whole works to a good finish, and slide the clear plastic sheet into place.

Fig. 8-11. Make two parallel saw cuts, and then pare the waste back with the chisel.

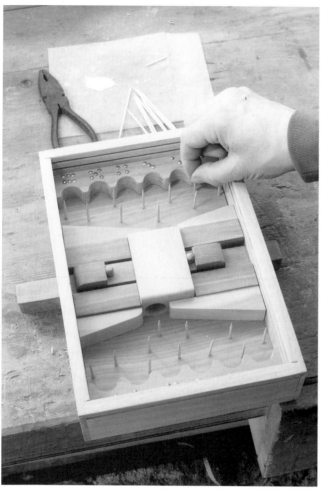

Fig. 8-12. Cut cocktail sticks to length and glue them in place.

Fig. 8-13. Test out the movement and the working action.

Afterthoughts and Troubleshooting

• The shuffler rod and the chamber block are at the heart of this project; they must be carefully cut and fitted. It's important to note that the order of work is slightly different in this project in that the bridge holes are cut in the box sides before the box is put together.

• Another way to make the marble pockets is to drill a line of holes down the center of a 2-inch-wide strip, and then run the strip through on a band saw.

• The pattern of pin holes will relate to the size of your marbles. If you look closely at the illustrations, you will see that I messed up and needed to cut one of the pins away so that the marbles could roll freely into the chamber.

Project 9
....

A No-Nonsense, No-Purpose, Ball-Bearing Shifter Contraption

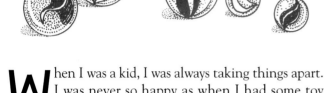

When I was a kid, I was always taking things apart. I was never so happy as when I had some toy or another dismantled. It's not so easy now, because so many toys and machines are sealed or made of plastic, but way back in the fifties, when it was all steel and nuts and bolts, there was no stopping kids like me.

Well, as I remember, my kid brother and I were both busy in the shed disassembling the back wheel of my bicycle—the object of the exercise being to find out why the three-speed gear hub did what it did—when suddenly the hub of the wheel popped off, and we were up to our white collars in an oily mess of screws, shims, springs, sprockets, spur wheels, studs, stays, square threads, and ball bearings. I don't remember much more, other than the horrible sweat of trying to pack all the parts back into the hub before school. It wasn't easy, and from then on, I was reduced to having a difficult-to-ride cycle with a fixed wheel, no gears, and a squeak—but we sure had had fun! This experience was likely what inspired this project.

This is a wonderful contraption to watch in action. All you do is wind the control wheel around until the arm on the main wheel engages in the slotted wheel, continue turning until one of the wheel slots is in line with the exit shaft on the top maze, and then joggle the box this way and that until one or more ball bearings run down the shaft and into the slot. At this point, you continue turning the control wheel so that the slotted wheel turns in a counterclockwise direction and delivers the ball bearing into the bottom maze. You repeat this procedure until all the balls are in the lower maze. Of course, it isn't easy, and the balls often get stuck and generally gum up the works, but it certainly is a wonderful contraption to watch in action. And just in case you're wondering if the arm-drive wheel and the slotted wheel ever get out kilter and grind to a halt, the answer is yes. But not to worry; if this happens, you simply push a little cocktail stick through a hole that you've drilled through the clear plastic sheet to one side of the slotted wheel and prod the workings back into action.

Design, Structure, and Techniques

If you are wondering why we are using ball bearings rather than marbles, all I can say in our defense is that we would have used small marbles if we could have found them. When we started designing, we quickly realized that a marble contraption with the same function would need to be much bigger, say 18 inches wide and 30 inches high. My advice, if you are determined to use marbles, is to make this project as a prototype, to sort out all the problems of scale and structure, and then move on to the big marble-running contraption at a later date.

It's interesting how this project evolved. We started with the notion of having the two wheels meshing, and we later came up with the idea of creating the movement by having the arm from one wheel locating in the slot of the other. If you look at the working drawings (see Figs. 9-1, 9-2, and 9-3), you will observe that it takes one complete revolution of the arm-drive wheel to turn the slotted wheel one notch. The arm goes around and then engages, and around again and engages, and so on. And each time the meshing takes place, the slotted wheel

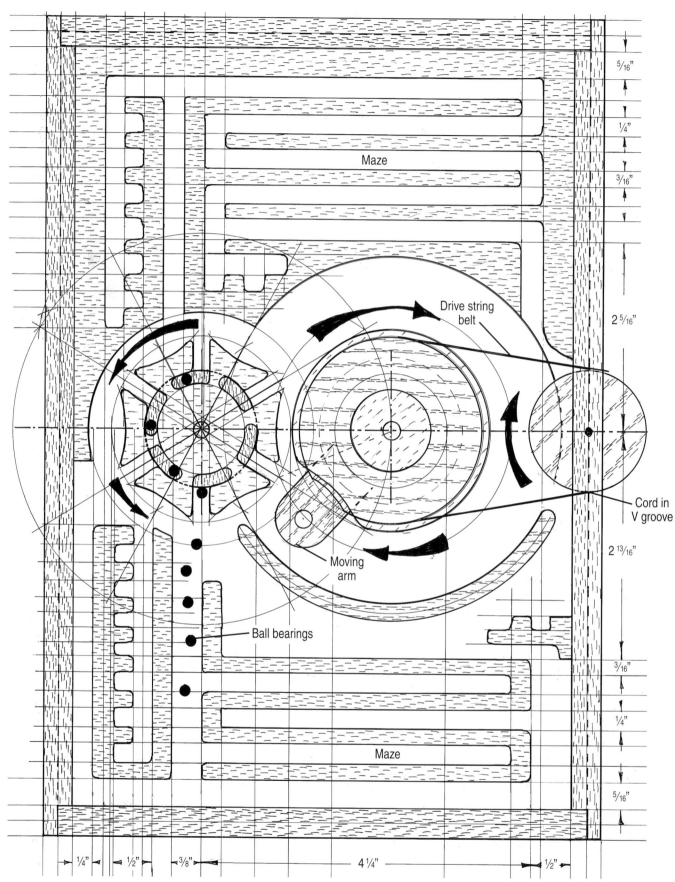

Maze

5/16"

1/4"

3/16"

2 5/16"

Drive string
belt

Cord in
V groove

2 13/16"

Moving
arm

Ball bearings

3/16"

1/4"

Maze

5/16"

1/4"   1/2"   3/8"   4 1/4"   1/2"

Fig. 9-1. The plan view, with all the component parts in place. Note all the extended lines around the slotted wheel; these are to be used as a guide for layout.

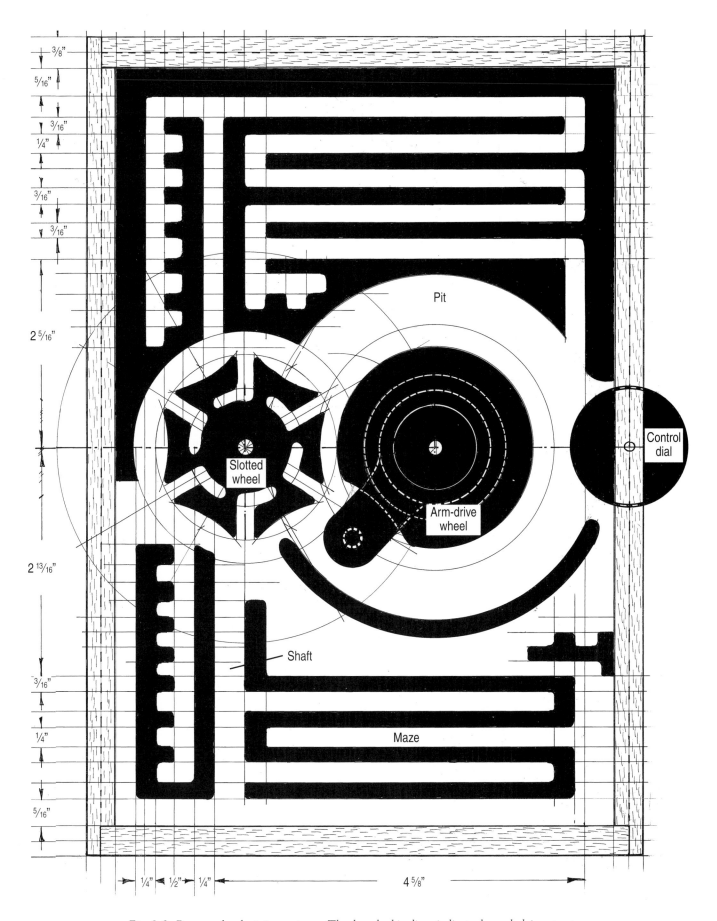

Fig. 9-2. Patterns for the primary parts. The dotted white lines indicate the underlying structure.

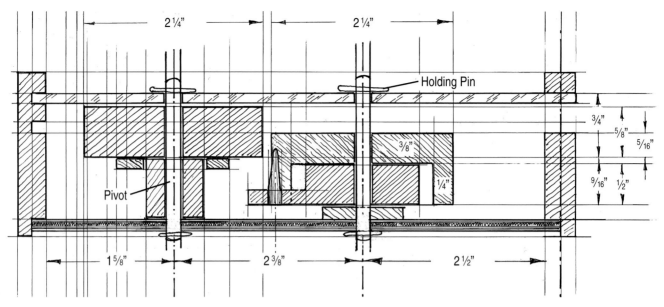

Fig. 9-3. A cross-section view showing how the slotted wheel and the arm-drive wheel relate to each other. Note how both wheels need to be lifted up from the base by a number of spacer disks.

moves one slot forward. Or to put it another way, it takes six revolutions of the arm-drive wheel to turn the slotted wheel one complete revolution. Though the wheels can be turned in either direction, the carrying and delivering action of the slotted wheel is better if it goes in a counterclockwise direction.

The movement is beautifully direct. With the contraption set upright, you turn the control dial, the dial starts the string belt moving, the string belt turns the arm-drive wheel, the arm-drive wheel revolves on its pivot, the moving arm engages in the slotted wheel, and the slotted wheel turns. As the slotted wheel revolves counterclockwise, it carries its load of ball bearings and delivers them one at a time into the bottom shaft and on into the maze.

When making the slotted wheel, I soon came to realize that not only was the wheel going to break up, what with the slots, short grain, and all, but more than that, the ball bearings were going to fall out the back of the slots. I solved this knotty little problem by gluing a thin disk to the back of the slotted wheel to act as a structural support and also to contain the balls.

The design of the maze is interesting. We were originally going to have two identical designs, one on top and the other on the bottom, but after fretting out the first maze, we were so taken by the complexity of the pieces of waste that we decided to use them as the other maze. So you see, you get two for the price of one—and that can't be bad!

Though this project involves wood turning, as the main cupped form of the arm-drive wheel is turned, it really is about working on the scroll saw. You have to have an electric scroll saw, and you most definitely have to enjoy working on an itsy-bitsy, finger-twitching scale. The making stages will involve you in a great deal of trial and error and experimentation. For example, when you get to sort out the meshing of the two wheels, you will have to set the wheels up on a trial rig to sort out the precise position of the pivot centers (see Figs. 9-7 and 9-11). Your wheels will be slightly larger or smaller than mine, so you will need to adjust the spacing of the pivots accordingly. Be prepared to spend a lot of time fiddling with the placement of the parts in relation to one another.

Choosing the Wood

Of all the projects so far in the book, this one calls for the widest range of wood. For example, the arm-drive wheel must be made from a close-grained easy-to-turn wood, the slotted wheel must be strong and stable across areas of short grain, and the maze must be strong and dense in all directions. Certainly, you could make the whole works from beech, but the project looks much more attractive if you make the various parts from contrasting woods. We chose to use ¾-inch-thick American cherry for the base slab and maze, 1-inch-thick European beech for the arm-drive wheel, ¾-inch-thick beech for the slotted wheel, ¼-inch-thick larch for the two V-groove drive-belt wheels, and odds and ends for the small component parts.

Making the Project
Cutting the Slotted Ball-Bearing Wheel

1. Take a good, long look at the working drawings (see Figs. 9-1, 9-2, and 9-3), and note how the design of the slotted wheel is based on a hexagon that is in turn based on a 2¼-inch-diameter circle. Be aware that the width of the slots will relate to your choice of ball bearings.

2. When you have studied the design in detail, and maybe even done some sketching yourself, take your chosen piece of ¾-inch-thick wood, fix your compass or dividers to a radius of ⅝ inch, and lay out the 1¼-inch-diameter circle. Step the ⅝-inch radius measurement around the circumference, and run lines from the resulting arc intersections through to the center point. Link the intersections to achieve a regular hexagon.

3. Mark the center points of the straight sides, then run straight lines from the center point of the circle through the midway points on the straight sides, so that the circle is divided into twelve equal segments. Use this framework to draw all the lines that go to make up the design (see Figs. 9-1, 9-2, and 9-3). If all that sounds like a pain, you can photocopy our working drawing and trace and pencil-transfer the imagery directly onto the wood.

4. Once the design is crisply laid out, set up the drill with a ¼-inch-diameter Forstner bit and sink six holes.

5. Move to the scroll saw, and fret out the shape of the wheel (see Fig. 9-4). The secret here is to go at it very gently, all the while doing your best to ensure that the wood doesn't split across areas of short grain. If you look closely at the run of the grain in relationship to the holes, you will see that as the pattern of six slots moves around the circle, at least two of the six thin necks are very short grained.

6. Use a scrap of fine-grade sandpaper to rub the fretted wheel down to a smooth finish.

Making the Arm-Drive Wheel

1. If you look at the working drawings (see Figs. 9-1, 9-2, and 9-3), you will see that the arm-drive wheel is made up of five component parts: the turned cup, the arm that fits within the cup, a little disk that fits underneath the arm to raise it up slightly from the base, the V-drive wheel that sits on top of the whole works, and the peg. Feel free to change the design some, if you so desire, and to use different tools.

2. To make the cup, take the 1-inch piece of wood, draw out the 2¼-inch-diameter blank, mount it on the lathe, and turn out the cup form. Have the walls ¼ inch thick and the base about ⅜ inch thick.

3. Drill a ¼-inch-diameter hole through the center for the pivot, cut the curve out on the scroll saw, and then use a chisel to pare the sawn ends to the walls back to a nicely rounded finish (see Fig. 9-5).

4. Take the ½-inch-thick wood that you have chosen for the arm, cut it to shape on the scroll saw, so that you finish up with a paddle-shaped piece that fits inside the cup, and then use a large-diameter Forstner bit to lower the peg step (see Fig. 9-6). Use a ¼-inch-diameter drill bit to sink the two holes, one for the pivot and the other for the drive peg.

Establishing the Position of the Drive Peg and Pivots

1. Once you have made the arm-drive wheel and the slotted wheel, now comes the difficulty of establishing the precise distance that the pivots need to be apart. Start by looking at the working drawing to see how the two wheels relate to each other. Then use three large

Fig. 9-4. When you are fretting out the slotted wheel, be very careful that you don't force the pace or put too much pressure on the fragile structure.

Fig. 9-5. *Use a small chisel to shape the wall to a rounded finish.*

4-inch nails to build a little test rig. Fix one of the two wheels in place on a slab of waste wood, and then experiment with the movement and turning circle (see Fig. 9-7).

2. When you have achieved a smooth movement, with the drive peg nicely engaging in the slots, then look at the various thicknesses and make a thin disk to fit underneath the arm so as to raise the whole arm-drive wheel up off the bottom of the box (see Fig. 9-3).

Fretting the Base Slab

1. When you are satisfied with the movement and have established the spacing of the pivot points, take the ¾-inch wood that you have chosen for the base slab and bring it to a perfect fit and finish, so that it drops neatly into the box.

2. Draw a pivot line that runs across the width of the slab, decide where on that line you want the wheels to be set, and then use a pair of compasses to draw in the two pits. Spike the point of the compass on the arm-drive wheel pivot, increase the radius from 1⅛ inches to about 2¼ inches, and scribe a circle. Do much the same with the compass on the slotted wheel pivot point, only this time around, increase the radius by about ⅛ inch (see Fig. 9-1).

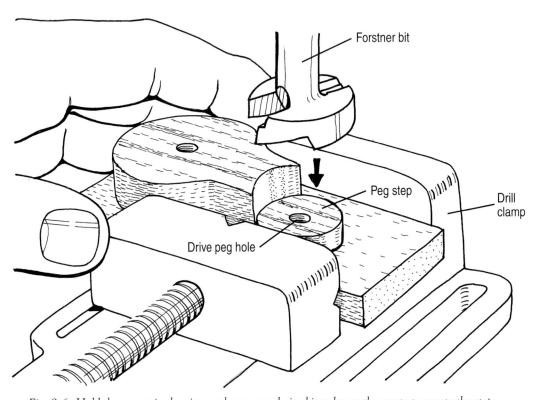

Fig. 9-6. *Hold the cutout in the vise, and use a good-size bit to lower the waste to create the step.*

Fig. 9-7. Set the two wheels up on a test rig, and see how they mesh with one another. Make adjustments to the slots and the spacing until it all works out.

Fig. 9-8. Cut the pit in the base slab, so that both wheels are nicely contained. The slotted wheel needs to be a close fit—not touching, but close.

3.   When you have the shape of the pit, like a large figure eight, then move to the scroll saw and clear the waste (see Fig. 9-8). Note how I used two pieces of wood to make the total slab shape.

4.   Rub the cut edges down to a smooth finish, and drop the slab into the box.

Fretting the Maze Slab

1.   Take the ¾-inch-thick slab you have chosen for the maze, and cut it to fit the box.

2.   Transfer the shape of the figure-eight pit through to the slab, then spend time drawing in the shape of the maze to fit. The shape of the maze isn't too important, other than that it needs to be as intricate as possible.

3.   When you are happy with the imagery, move to the scroll saw and spend time quietly fretting out the design. Start with a new blade, make sure that it is well tensioned, work at an easy pace, and do your best to run the line of cut to the waste side of the drawn line (see Fig. 9-9).

Making the V-Drive Wheels

1.   The good news here is that after all the difficulties of making the two meshing wheels, the V-drive wheels are very easy to construct. Start by drawing out the two disks, one about 2⅛ inches in diameter, and the other about 1½ inches.

2.   When you've cut the wheels out on the scroll saw, run the small dial wheel through with a ¹⁄₁₆-inch-diameter bit, so that the hole is just big enough for the steel pin pivot, and the other wheel through with a ¾-

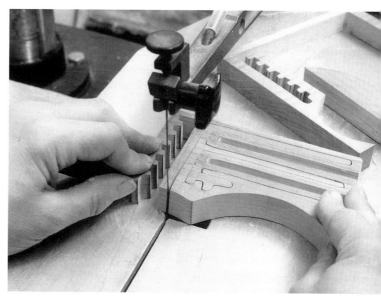

Fig. 9-9. If you fit a new blade and go at it slowly, the cut edge will require only a minimum of sanding.

inch-diameter bit, so that there is enough room for the wooden pin to be pushed sideways through the pivot.

3.   Run a pencil line around the sawn edge of the wheels, to split the ¼-inch width in half, then take a triangular section file and work along the line cutting in the V-shaped trench (see Fig. 9-10).

4.   Go around and around until you have a well-defined groove, and then rub it down to a good finish.

5.   Set the wheels on the trial jig and see how they fit and relate to the slotted wheel and the arm-drive wheel

Fig. 9-10. Run the V-riffler file repeatedly around the edge until you have a V-section groove for the drive cord.

Fig. 9-11. See how I needed to shape the drive peg at the end of the drive arm.

(see Fig. 9-11), then move to the scroll saw and remove the little "bite" from the side of the large V-drive wheel.

Perfecting the Movement and Final Assembly

1. Of all the projects in the book, this one requires the most fitting. The problem is that things change at every stage. So even though you think you've sorted out the problems at the trial-rig stage, you'll almost certainly have to keep modifying right up until the end.

2. Having put the box together and fitted the plywood base sheet (see the section on Making the Basic Box), mark in the position of the dial wheel slot on the outside face of one long side. Run two ¾-inch-diameter holes through the waste (see Fig. 9-12), clear the rest with a hand coping saw, and then rub the sawn edges down to a smooth finish.

3. When you've made all the component parts, start by gluing the base slab in place in the box.

4. Next, glue the maze in place on the base slab, the arm inside the turned cup that goes to make the arm-drive wheel, and the large V-drive wheel in place on top of the arm-drive wheel.

5. Drill the two pivot holes through the bottom of the box, set the pivots in place, and then, not forgetting the various distancing disks, set the two wheels on the pivots (see Fig. 9-13).

6. And so you continue, popping a nail down into the thickness of the box wall to pivot the dial wheel on, putting little wooden pegs through both ends of the pivots so that they are held in place, and so on. Continue until all the parts are installed.

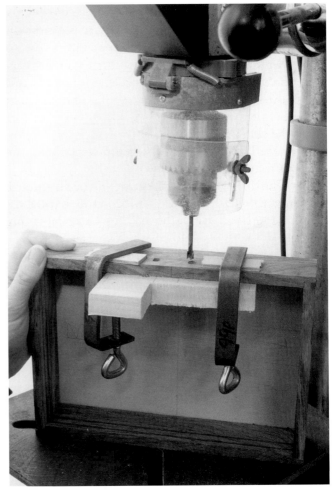

Fig. 9-12. Have a good-size chunk of waste wood clamped to the inside of the box to prevent the drill bit from splitting the wood as it exits.

7. Wax and polish all the surfaces to a sheen finish.

8. Run the waxed cord around the two V-drive wheels, and tie them off with a sliding knot. Drop a handful of ball bearings into the box.

9. Take the clear plastic sheet, in which you've made three holes—two pivot holes and the "prodding" hole—remove the holding pins from the two pivot rods, and lower the rods slightly by retracting them from the underside of the base so that you can slide the plastic in place in the box.

10. Slide the pivots back up from the underside of the box so that you can push the holding pins back in place through the pivots. Finally, ease the drive string around until the sliding knot is on the outside of the box, and then tighten up, make the knot fast, and trim.

Afterthoughts and Troubleshooting

• Although we have given a good number of measurements on the working drawings, we have not provided them all. Our thinking is that if you have made it this far in the book, you will be so experienced in the art of making marble contraptions that you will almost certainly want to go your own way and make variations of your own.

• We have to admit here that although this contraption is the most exciting visually, it is hell to make. It's not that any particular component is difficult to construct, but rather that all the little fidgeting and fiddling with the cord and the movement will put your patience to the test. That said, it is well worth the effort; the movement is truly fascinating.

• The drive cord was something of a problem. After experimenting with many different kinds of twine and cord, we settled on waxed thread. The slight stickiness

Fig. 9-13. Set the dial wheel in the slot, and pivot it on a steel nail.

of the wax makes for a good, high-friction grip on the V-drive wheels, and the wax protects the thread from atmospheric changes so that it won't get damp and slacken off.

• Do your very best to make sure that the contents of the box are at a slightly lower level than the underside of the top groove. If you aren't careful, the components will rub against the underside of the plastic sheet when you are sliding it in place and damage the soft plastic.

• Having the pivots sticking out at each side of the box—through the base and through the plastic—is no problem, because the box is designed to be used while standing on end.

The Magnificent Goldberg-Robinson-Williamson Marble-Kicking Device

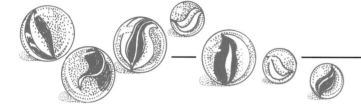

This project draws its inspiration from, and is dedicated to, three wonderful characters: William Heath Robinson, English illustrator and genius; Reuben Lucius Goldberg, American cartoonist and genius; and Arthur George Williamson, my grandpa and friend. Just what did these three guys have in common? They always took the roundabout route to getting a job done. Give them a seemingly simple task, like washing a plate or closing a gate, and they would start building a contraption to get the task done with more speed and less effort. Or should I say less speed and more effort? The only difference between my grandpa and the other two guys is that though the latter were getting paid good money for their quirky-weird-wonderful designs, my grandpa was simply a lovable, one-of-a-kind sort of chap who truly believed his devices were the answer. His gate-closing contraption involved using four yards of best-quality catgut, two little clamps, three brass pulley wheels saved from the wreck of a small sailing dinghy, a medium-size galvanized bucket, two and half house bricks, and a large spring salvaged from an old, wind-up gramophone. The gate device was great! The trick was being quick enough to get through before the mechanism started to grind unstoppably into action.

The marble-kicking contraption is truly a device for doing nothing fast. If you want to waste several precious days building a contraption that at the very best will draw a laugh from your friends and ridicule from your enemies, this is the project for you. If you were to ask me what it does, I would have to say . . . not a lot. Okay, so all the strings and pulleys do most cleverly move into

action when the lever is pulled down, and the boot does kick upward, and all the rest, but as for the bell ringing or the boot getting to kick the marble, no way!

The thing that you have to bear in mind with this cunningly sly little work of genius is that its utter pointlessness is the whole point. Or to put it another way, if it draws a laugh and your friends chide you for its inanity, then it has perfectly performed its function.

Design, Structure, and Techniques

Take a good, long look at the design (see Figs. 10-1, 10-2, and 10-3), and consider how the whole contraption is a play on the use of levers, pulleys, springs, and cords. As for engineering concepts behind the design, all you really have to remember is that when you pull down on one end of a seesaw lever, the other end goes up. And of course, when the end that goes up starts pulling on other levers and strings that in turn pull on still other levers and strings, there is a series of cause-and-effect actions. As for the function of the other gizmos, the pulley guides redirect the strings, and the springs pull all the strings and levers back into the starting position.

Study the working drawings, follow through all the working stages, take note of the various techniques, sort around your workshop for likely looking items, and then get building!

Choosing the Wood

Apart from the box itself, and the ¾-inch-thick base slab, all you really need is a good, long length of ¼-inch-diameter dowel, a couple of ⅛-inch-diameter barbecue

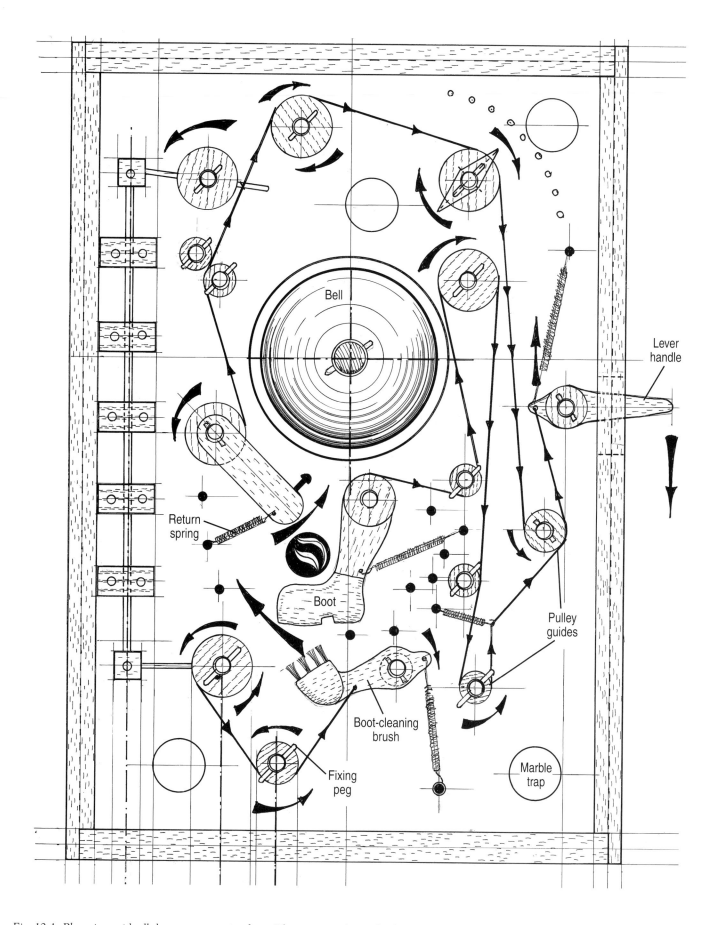

Fig. 10-1. Plan view with all the components in place. The arrows indicate the direction of movement when the control lever is pulled down.

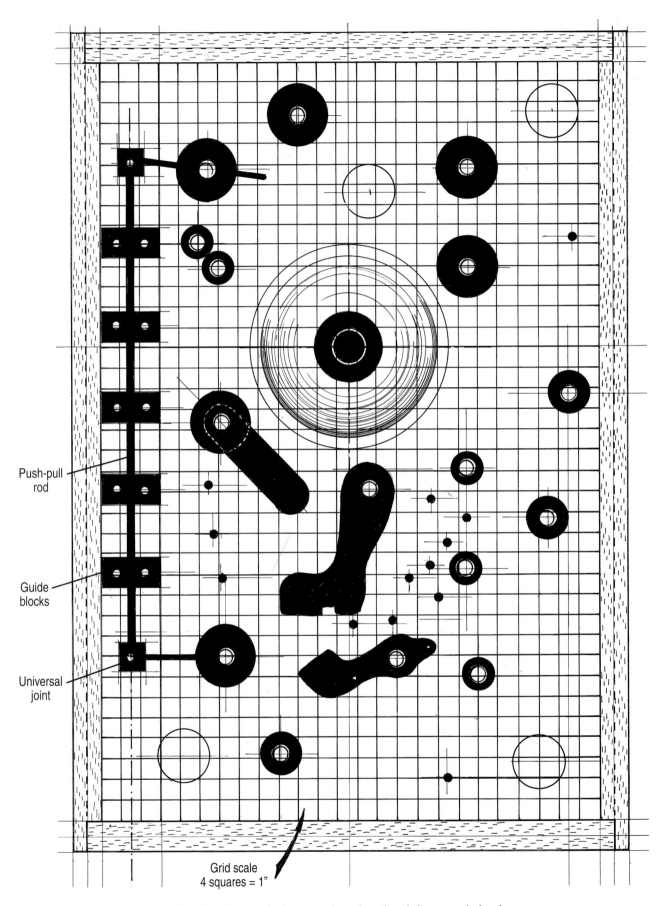

Push-pull rod

Guide blocks

Universal joint

Grid scale
4 squares = 1"

Fig. 10-2. Patterns laid out on a ¼-inch grid, to help you with the placing.

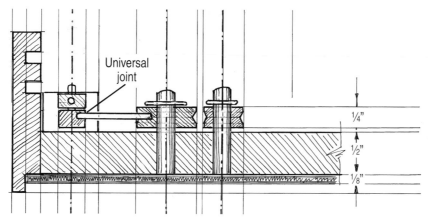

Fig. 10-3.Cross-section detail showing how the two pulley wheels at bottom left relate to each other and to the universal joint at the bottom of the push-pull rod.

sticks, a handful of small-diameter cocktail sticks, a length of 1-inch-square-section wood for the turned pulleys, and lots of small pieces of dense-grained wood for all the other odds and ends. We used a piece of beachcombed mahogany for the base slab, oak for the pulleys, beech for the levers, and lime and pine for the small blocks.

Special Tip

You can save money on the wood, by keeping your eyes open for used wood that can be salvaged. There are enormous quantities of it out there: oak and pine floorboards from houses that are being pulled down, all manner of wood from beachcombing, oak and beech from old furniture, good-quality plywood from furniture and packing cases, scrap wood from window and door manufacturers—the list goes on. And then again, the whole idea of using salvaged parts is in keeping with the Goldberg-Robinson-Williamson (and Bridgewater) philosophy. If, for example, you can disassemble the printer ribbon holder from your computer printer, and use the little cog wheels in one or another of the projects, then so much the better.

Making the Project
Turning the Pulleys

1. Study the working drawings (see Figs. 10-1, 10-2, and 10-3) and decide whether you want to make any variations for your own contraption. Then estimate how many pulley wheels you need, adding some if you wish. Make allowances for breakage and different sizes. We used two different sizes—¾ inch and ½ inch diameter—but if you want, you can go for a whole range of sizes.

Note how we used the same 1-inch-square-section length of wood for both diameters.

2. Mount the wood on a lathe, and swiftly turn it down to a smooth ¾-inch-diameter cylinder.

3. Set your dividers to ¼ inch, and then work along the cylinder, laying it out with a good number of ¼-inch set-offs: ¼ inch for parting waste, ¼ inch for the first pulley, ¼ inch for parting waste, and so on along the length of the wood. And if you need a special form to hold a bell or whatever, then lay this out along the way.

4. Use the parting tool to reduce the diameter of selected step-offs for the smaller pulleys.

5. Use the tool of your choice to give each ¼-inch pulley step-off a V-groove for the cord. You could use the toe of a skew chisel, a V-shaped scraper, or even the corner of the parting tool (see Fig. 10-4).

Fig. 10-4. Tidy up the pulley wheels with the toe of a skew chisel, and then part off.

Fig. 10-5. *A length of block section ready to be sawn into lengths and a sawn length being tested for size and fit. The tracing shows our first, unmodified design.*

6. Sand to a good finish and part off.

7. Drill a pivot hole through each of the pulleys with a bit size to match your chosen dowel diameter.

Making the Blocks and Rods

1. Take a look at the working drawings (see Figs. 10-1, 10-2, and 10-3), decide on the sizes of the blocks, and then plane your chosen wood to size. We used a ½-by-⅜-inch section for the long blocks that hold the push-and-pull rod and a ⁷⁄₁₆-by-¼-inch section for the small, square universal joint blocks.

2. Use a square and rule to mark the length of the block sizes. Decide where the holes for the pins, pegs and rods need to be, and then run them through with the appropriate bits.

3. Cut the blocks to length, and test-fit. The push-and-pull rod needs to be an easy, smooth-sliding fit, whereas the fixing pegs need to be a tight push-fit (see Fig. 10-5).

4. Once you've sized and drilled the various blocks, try out a typical movement—say, the pulley wheel with a through rod that links up to the push-and-pull rod—and see how it works out (see Fig. 10-6). Try out the components for size and movement, and if you need to make modifications, now is the time to do it.

Drilling the Base Slab and Fixing the Dowel Pivots and Pulley Wheels

1. There are two ways of approaching this project. You can either draw every last dot and dash out on tracing paper and then painstakingly press-transfer the details onto the slab, or you can use a square and rule to draw the details and then fine-tune as you go along. If at the end you have too many holes, then you just add another pulley or decorative detail. For example, we drilled the large holes for the trapped marbles to cover a blunder.

2. When you have established the position of the main pivot holes on the base slab, and perhaps a large feature like the bell, run them through with the appropriate-size drill bits.

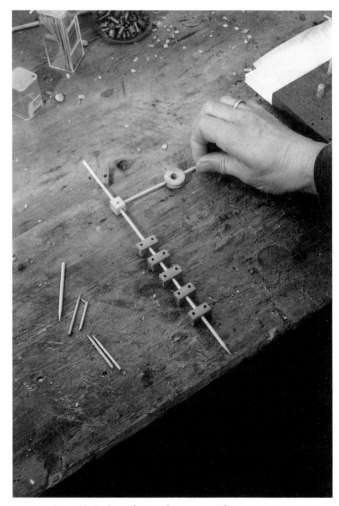

Fig. 10-6. *Spend time fine-tuning the movement.*

Fig. 10-7. Drill the pattern of holes, and set the main pivots in position. A tight-fitting hole for a cocktail stick has been drilled across the width of each pivot.

3. Cross-drill the pivots so that they can take a little holding pin, then systematically glue them in place in the base slab (see Fig. 10-7).

4. Set the pulley wheels on the pivots, the bell on its stem, the boot on its pivot, and so on (see Fig. 10-8).

5. Slide the control lever in place on its pivot so that there is about 1 inch of lever extending through to the outside of the box.

Threading Up the Cords

1. When you have set up a cluster of pulley wheels, then take a length of cord and have a trial threading up. Pull the control lever down, experiment with various arrangements, and see how they perform (see Fig. 10-9).

2. If at any point along the way you find that some part of your drawn design doesn't work, be ready to change it. For example, a pull-and-push rod originally intended for the top right of the device (see Fig. 10-9, top right of the tracing) just didn't work, so we used a couple of extra pulleys instead.

3. And so you continue, putting the pulley wheels on the pivot, setting the blocks in place, threading up a bit more of the system, and so on, until you have achieved a good movement. Aim for a tight push-fit for the little wooden holding pegs (see Fig. 10-10).

Fitting the Springs and Final Assembly

1. Take a look at the working drawings (see Figs. 10-1, 10-2, and 10-3) and the various photographs, and consider how the function of all the springs is to assist the overall movement by pulling. There are no pushing strings. Though the first cluster of pulley wheels needs

Fig. 10-8. Fitting some of the cords was difficult.

Fig. 10-9. Keeping in mind that all that's required is that the boot kick up when the lever is pulled down, experiment with various cording patterns.

Fig. 10-10. Ideally, the little wooden pins need to be a tight push-fit. It's best not to glue them until the very last moment.

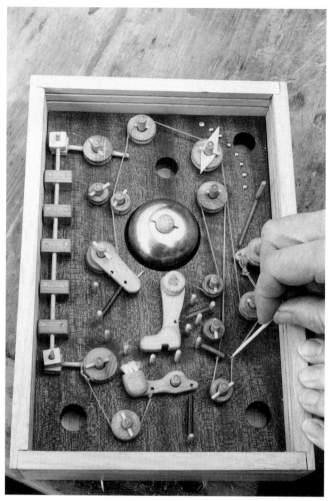

Fig. 10-11. Here the spring is hooked to the cord to keep the cord tight.

Fig. 10-12. Use a needle to help you tie on the cords.

Fig. 10-13. Detail showing the size of the slot in relationship to the lever.

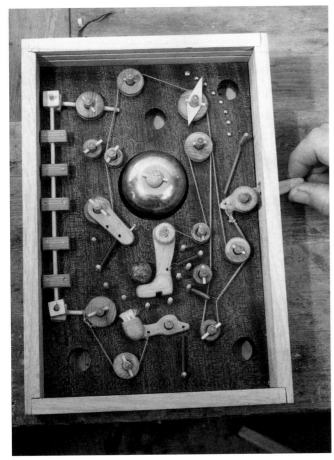

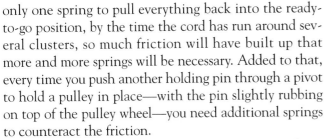

Fig. 10-14. Position of the component parts when the lever is in the ready-to-go mode.

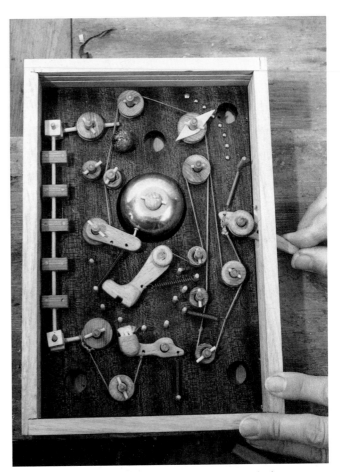

Fig. 10-15. Position of the component parts when the lever is in the down mode.

only one spring to pull everything back into the ready-to-go position, by the time the cord has run around several clusters, so much friction will have built up that more and more springs will be necessary. Added to that, every time you push another holding pin through a pivot to hold a pulley in place—with the pin slightly rubbing on top of the pulley wheel—you need additional springs to counteract the friction.

2. In some instances it helps the movement if you have a spring running from a peg directly to the cord to correct the tension (see Fig. 10-11).

3. Fixing the cord can be a problem, as the knots need to be tight. Use an upholstery needle to thread the cord through the difficult holes (see Fig. 10-12).

4. Though we originally had the pulley wheel on the control lever pivot for decorative effect and to act as a loose washer, we eventually decided to strengthen the lever by gluing the wheel to its upper surface (see Fig. 10-13).

5. Once you have the entire device assembled, with the knots glued and all the surfaces waxed, have a try-out and see how it goes (see Figs. 10-14 and 10-15).

6. Once everything is working smoothly, pop the marble in position, slide the clear plastic sheet in place, and you're ready to go.

Afterthoughts and Troubleshooting

• In many ways, this project was problematic because I continually had to drill new pivot holes. It probably would have made things a lot easier if I had started by laying out an overall pattern of pivot holes on the base slab. I could have drawn out a 1/4-inch grid and then had pivot holes at every intersection.

• The choice of cords was a problem. Though there are any number of strong nylon cords to be had, they are all flawed in that not only do they have a tendency to fray and unravel, but worse still, they are so slippery that they can't be tied. Nevertheless, the best choice is waxed linen thread or cord.

• It was difficult to find springs of the correct slack and easy type. In the end, I purchased them via mail order from a model-making magazine. I believe they were originally designed for use in light electronic goods such as tape players.

Metric Conversions

INCHES TO MILLIMETERS

in.	mm	in.	mm
1	25.4	51	1295.4
2	50.8	52	1320.8
3	76.2	53	1346.2
4	101.6	54	1371.6
5	127.0	55	1397.0
6	152.4	56	1422.4
7	177.8	57	1447.8
8	203.2	58	1473.2
9	228.6	59	1498.6
10	254.0	60	1524.0
11	279.4	61	1549.4
12	304.8	62	1574.8
13	330.2	63	1600.2
14	355.6	64	1625.6
15	381.0	65	1651.0
16	406.4	66	1676.4
17	431.8	67	1701.8
18	457.2	68	1727.2
19	482.6	69	1752.6
20	508.0	70	1778.0
21	533.4	71	1803.4
22	558.8	72	1828.8
23	584.2	73	1854.2
24	609.6	74	1879.6
25	635.0	75	1905.0
26	660.4	76	1930.4
27	685.8	77	1955.8
28	711.2	78	1981.2
29	736.6	79	2006.6
30	762.0	80	2032.0
31	787.4	81	2057.4
32	812.8	82	2082.8
33	838.2	83	2108.2
34	863.6	84	2133.6
35	889.0	85	2159.0
36	914.4	86	2184.4
37	939.8	87	2209.8
38	965.2	88	2235.2
39	990.6	89	2260.6
40	1016.0	90	2286.0
41	1041.4	91	2311.4
42	1066.8	92	2336.8
43	1092.2	93	2362.2
44	1117.6	94	2387.6
45	1143.0	95	2413.0
46	1168.4	96	2438.4
47	1193.8	97	2463.8
48	1219.2	98	2489.2
49	1244.6	99	2514.6
50	1270.0	100	2540.0

The above table is exact on the basis: 1 in. = 25.4 mm

U.S. TO METRIC

1 inch = 2.540 centimeters
1 foot = .305 meter
1 yard = .914 meter
1 mile = 1.609 kilometers

METRIC TO U.S.

1 millimeter = .039 inch
1 centimeter = .394 inch
1 meter = 3.281 feet or 1.094 yards
1 kilometer = .621 mile

INCH-METRIC EQUIVALENTS

Fraction	Customary (in.)	Metric (mm)	Fraction	Customary (in.)	Metric (mm)
1/64	.015	0.3969	33/64	.515	13.0969
1/32	.031	0.7938	17/32	.531	13.4938
3/64	.046	1.1906	35/64	.546	13.8906
1/16	.062	1.5875	9/16	.562	14.2875
5/64	.078	1.9844	37/64	.578	14.6844
3/32	.093	2.3813	19/32	.593	15.0813
7/64	.109	2.7781	39/64	.609	15.4781
1/8	.125	3.1750	5/8	.625	15.8750
9/64	.140	3.5719	41/64	.640	16.2719
5/32	.156	3.9688	21/32	.656	16.6688
11/64	.171	4.3656	43/64	.671	17.0656
3/16	.187	4.7625	11/16	.687	17.4625
13/64	.203	5.1594	45/64	.703	17.8594
7/32	.218	5.5563	23/32	.718	18.2563
15/64	.234	5.9531	47/64	.734	18.6531
1/4	.250	6.3500	3/4	.750	19.0500
17/64	.265	6.7469	49/64	.765	19.4469
9/32	.281	7.1438	25/32	.781	19.8438
19/64	.296	7.5406	51/64	.796	20.2406
5/16	.312	7.9375	13/16	.812	20.6375
21/64	.328	8.3384	53/64	.828	21.0344
11/32	.343	8.7313	27/32	.843	21.4313
23/64	.359	9.1281	55/64	.859	21.8281
3/8	.375	9.5250	7/8	.875	22.2250
25/64	.390	9.9219	57/64	.890	22.6219
13/32	.406	10.3188	29/32	.906	23.0188
27/64	.421	10.7156	59/64	.921	23.4156
7/16	.437	11.1125	15/16	.937	23.8125
29/64	.453	11.5094	61/64	.953	24.2094
15/32	.468	11.9063	31/32	.968	24.6063
31/64	.484	12.3031	63/64	.984	25.0031
1/2	.500	12.7000	1	1.000	25.4000